Jossey-Bass Teacher

Jossey-Bass Teacher provides educators with practical knowledge and tools to create a positive and lifelong impact on student learning. We offer classroom-tested and research-based teaching resources for a variety of grade levels and subject areas. Whether you are an aspiring, new, or veteran teacher, we want to help you make every teaching day your best.

From ready-to-use classroom activities to the latest teaching framework, our value-packed books provide insightful, practical, and comprehensive materials on the topics that matter most to K–12 teachers. We hope to become your trusted source for the best ideas from the most experienced and respected experts in the field.

More Praise for Collaborative Strategic Reading and *NOW WE GET IT!*

" *We are so fortunate to work with CSR in our schools—our teachers have seen student comprehension increase and the flexibility of the strategy lets all the teachers in a school work together as a team in increase achievement.* "

—SUSANA CORDOVA, CHIEF ACADEMIC OFFICER, DENVER PUBLIC SCHOOLS

" *CSR is a great tool for teachers, students and parents that can amplify literacy and comprehension skills across grade levels and content school wide!* "

—ANTHONY A. SMITH, PRINCIPAL, MARTIN LUTHER KING, JR. EARLY COLLEGE

" *Collaborative Strategic Reading is the most complete package of strategies for reading instruction that I have found. The collaborative structure helps students work through the before, during, and after reading framework to better comprehend information in any core subject area. Students in elementary and secondary grades can use these strategies and work together to become better readers.* "

—TERRY FIELDER, DIRECTOR, INTERVENTION SERVICES, HAYS CONSOLIDATED INDEPENDENT SCHOOL DISTRICT, TEXAS

Now We Get It!

Boosting Comprehension with Collaborative Strategic Reading

Janette Klingner
Sharon Vaughn
Alison Boardman
Elizabeth Swanson

JOSSEY-BASS
A Wiley Imprint
www.josseybass.com

Published by Jossey-Bass

A Wiley Imprint

One Montgomery Street, Suite 1200, San Francisco, CA 94104-4594—www.josseybass.com

The CSR professional development procedures and materials we describe in this book were developed with support from grant R305A080608 from the Institute of Education Sciences, US Department of Education. The content is solely the responsibility of the authors and does not necessarily represent the official views of the Institute of Education Sciences or the US Department of Education.

CSR Comprehension Strategies (p. 4) reprinted with permission from the Meadows Center for Preventing Educational Risk (2009). CSR strategies. Austin, TX: Janette Klingner and Sharon Vaughn.

Portions of CSR Comprehension Strategies ("Preview" on p. 5, "Click & Clunk" on p. 7, "Get the Gist" on p. 10, and "Wrap Up" on p. 12) adapted with permission from the Meadows Center for Preventing Educational Risk (2009). CSR strategies. Austin, TX: Janette Klingner and Sharon Vaughn.

Learning Log for Informational Text (pp. 142–143), Learning Log for Narrative Text (pp. 144–145) adapted with permission from the Meadows Center for Preventing Educational Risk (2009). CSR learning log for informational text. Austin, TX: Janette Klingner and Sharon Vaughn.

Student cue cards (pp. 146–152) adapted with permission from the Meadows Center for Preventing Educational Risk (2009). CSR student cue cards. Austin, TX: Janette Klingner and Sharon Vaughn.

Teacher cue cards (pp. 153–159) adapted with permission from the Meadows Center for Preventing Educational Risk (2009). CSR teacher cue cards. Austin, TX: Janette Klingner and Sharon Vaughn.

Library of Congress Cataloging-in-Publication Data

Now we get it! : boosting comprehension with collaborative strategic reading / Janette K. Klingner . . . [et al.].—1st ed.

　　p. cm.—(Jossey-Bass teacher)

　　Includes bibliographical references and index.

　　ISBN 978-1-118-02609-0 (pbk.)

　　1. Mixed ability grouping in education–United States.　　2. Reading–United States.　　3. Reading comprehension.　　4. Classroom management–United States.　　I. Klingner, Janette K.

　　LB3061.3.H68 2012

　　372.470973–dc23

　　　　　　　　　　　　2012001572

ABOUT THE AUTHORS

Janette Klingner, PhD, is professor of education at the University of Colorado, Boulder. A former bilingual special education teacher, she focuses her current research on two main areas: reading comprehension strategy instruction for culturally and linguistically diverse students and Response to Intervention for English language learners. To date she has authored or coauthored more than one hundred articles, books, and book chapters, and has presented at numerous national and international conferences, frequently as a keynote speaker.

Sharon Vaughn, PhD, is the H. E. Hartfelder/Southland Corp. Regents Chair and executive director of the Meadows Center for Preventing Educational Risk (MCPER) at the University of Texas. An internationally known expert on the reading and social outcomes of students with learning disabilities and English language learners, she was the previous editor of *Journal of Learning Disabilities* and coeditor of *Learning Disabilities Research & Practice*. She is the author of more than ten books and more than 150 articles.

Alison Boardman, PhD, is an assistant research professor at the University of Colorado, Boulder. She is the co-principal investigator of a US Department of Education–funded grant to study the schoolwide use of Collaborative Strategic Reading (CSR) in urban middle schools. A former elementary and middle school special educator, she has extensive experience providing professional development to teachers across the United States to successfully teach comprehension strategies in their classrooms.

Elizabeth Swanson, PhD, is a research assistant professor at the University of Texas at Austin, where she is also a lead researcher at the Meadows Center for Preventing Educational Risk. She is currently the co-principal investigator on a series of studies sponsored through the Reading for Understanding initiative funded by the Institute of Education Sciences (IES), investigating the prevention and remediation of reading comprehension difficulties among students in seventh through twelfth grades.

We dedicate this book to the many teachers, principals, and students in the school districts in which we have worked: Del Valle Independent School District (Texas), Denver Public Schools (Colorado), Hays Independent School District (Texas), Jefferson County Public Schools (Colorado) and St. Vrain Valley School District (Colorado).

ACKNOWLEDGMENTS

We would like to acknowledge the wonderful teachers who have implemented CSR in their classrooms as part of our many research projects. Their insights have helped improve CSR to be what it is today. We also wish to thank the many members of our research teams who have provided invaluable support on our CSR projects over the last ten years, including (but not limited to) Estella Almanza de Schonewise, Subini Annamma, Maria Elena Argüelles, Amy Boelé, Steve Ciullo, Amy Eppolito, Christa Haring, Bindiya Hassaram, Marie Tejero Hughes, Suzette Leftwich, Lisa McCulley, Susan Miller-Curley, Colleen Reutebuch, Karla Scornavacco, Michael Solis, Stephanie Stillman, and Kathryn H. O. White.

CONTENTS

Now We Get It!

INTRODUCTION: COLLABORATIVE STRATEGIC READING IN A NUTSHELL

> *The fisherman of Minamata began protesting against Chisso Corporation in 1959. They demanded compensation, and that Chisso quit dumping toxic waste.*
>
> **—TEXT EXCERPT FROM A MIDDLE SCHOOL SCIENCE TEXTBOOK**

> *Daniel:* What does *compensate* mean?
>
> *Alex:* I am not sure, but I know what *recompensa* means in Spanish—it means to pay back someone when you hurt them.
>
> *Daniel:* Oh, so you think they wanted money from the company?
>
> *Alex:* Yeah, that makes sense. I guess it's pretty cool to be bilingual.
>
> **—STUDENTS IN A CSR GROUP**

Daniel and Alex are using CSR's Click and Clunk strategy to identify words they do not understand while reading and to take steps to figure out what they mean. They are working collaboratively in Collaborative Strategic Reading (CSR) cooperative learning groups. In this book, you will learn how to implement CSR and also how to teach others to use CSR.

This book has multiple purposes. First and foremost, it is intended to be used by teachers and professional developers who would like to implement CSR and instruct others on how to do so. But it also can be used by administrators, support personnel, and parents who have heard about CSR and wish to study it on their own, or perhaps who have participated in a CSR professional development workshop and would like to learn more about it.

In the 2001 book *Collaborative Strategic Reading*, which Janette and Sharon coauthored with Joe Dimino, Jeanne Schumm, and Diane Bryant,[1] we introduced CSR, presented the research base behind it at that time, and offered suggestions for using CSR in high school classrooms. In the years since, many changes have been made to CSR. The program has been fine-tuned after being implemented in diverse fourth-through eighth-grade classrooms across the country. We have learned a great deal from the many teachers who have participated in our research studies about how to use CSR during language arts, reading, science, and social studies lessons in feasible, effective ways. One of our primary goals in this book is to share those many changes and improvements to CSR.

Our second goal is to provide explicit instructions in how to conduct CSR professional development activities. We focus on what it takes to implement CSR well. Since 2001, we have revised how we provide professional development and how we support teachers' usage of CSR in their classrooms. Participants in our workshops and in our research studies have offered us valuable feedback that has enabled us to hone our professional development and coaching techniques. In a nutshell, in writing this book, we draw from almost twenty years of experience developing, fine-tuning, and teaching CSR.

An Overview of CSR

CSR is a research-based intervention that has been implemented successfully in culturally and linguistically diverse inclusive classrooms from fourth grade through middle school.[2] CSR includes strategies for monitoring comprehension, reviewing and synthesizing information, asking and answering questions, and taking steps to improve understanding. It also incorporates peer discussion.

CSR is divided into before-, during-, and after-reading activities. The Preview strategy is used before reading a designated text. The text can be multiple paragraphs or multiple pages but previewing occurs only once—prior to reading the entire selected text. The Click and Clunk and Gist strategies are used during reading and occur more frequently because they are applied to a one-, two-, or three-paragraph section of text. Thus, if the entire text is six paragraphs and the teacher has divided the passage into three sections of two paragraphs each, students would Preview once (before reading) and then Click and Clunk and Get the Gist three times. Wrap Up is like Preview in that it occurs only one time; however, it is used at the end of the six-paragraph text rather than the beginning. We like to think of Preview and Wrap Up as the bookend strategies with previewing occurring before students read and Wrap Up occurring after students read.

Before Reading: Preview

Before reading, the teacher and students *Preview* the text together to activate background knowledge, make connections between the day's topic and prior learning, predict what might be learned, and set a purpose for reading. During this phase, the teacher guides students to scan the title, headings, pictures, and charts or tables in the day's reading. The teacher prompts students to brainstorm what they already know about the topic and invites them to share their ideas with their classmates. The teacher helps students build background knowledge as needed and also introduces two or three key vocabulary terms and proper nouns. Teachers may use real objects, pictures, short video clips, or demonstrations to make connections explicit for students. Students then use the information provided to build background knowledge as well as to understand the text to make predictions about what they will learn. Finally, the teacher sets a purpose for reading. This purpose might relate to how the reading connects to the "big ideas" the students are learning in their unit of study or to a specific strategy the teacher wants them to pay particular attention to while using CSR.

During Reading: Click and Clunk and Get the Gist

During reading, students use a strategy called *Click and Clunk* to monitor comprehension and identify confusing words or concepts. When the text makes sense, it clicks; when it does not, it clunks. Once the students have finished a section, they apply fix-up strategies to the unknown words and concepts: (1) reread the sentence with the clunk in it and determine if they can find the meaning from the context clues; (2) reread the sentence with the clunk and the sentences before or after, looking for clues to help figure out the clunk; (3) break the word apart and look for a prefix, suffix, or a root word; and (4) look for a cognate that makes sense. In order to ensure the accuracy of the definition they have generated, students return to the text and insert the new definition to confirm that it makes sense.

After students repair their clunks, they move on to the Get the Gist phase, where they determine the main idea in the section of text they have just finished reading. This generally requires integrating information across multiple paragraphs in a longer section of text. Students first agree on the most important who or what in the section. Next they each write their own gist statements in their CSR learning logs and share them with one another. They are challenged to limit the word count of their main idea statements so they can condense only the most important information and avoid adding too many details. Students are encouraged to discuss the quality of each other's gists, providing evidence from the text to support their ideas. Groups sometimes come up with a "super gist" that takes into account the best aspects of multiple gists.

After Reading: Wrap Up

After reading, students *Wrap Up*. They do this by formulating and answering teacherlike questions about the text they have just read and by identifying the most important ideas in the passage. They try to think of easier and more challenging questions that require an understanding of the passage as well as connections with prior knowledge. Finally, students write down one or two of the most important ideas from the passage. They must be prepared to justify why they think their ideas are important.

CSR is distinctive in its emphasis on students co-constructing knowledge through peer discussion while working in cooperative groups in which each student learns to perform an expert role. The expert roles include Leader, Clunk Expert, Gist Expert, and Question Expert. These roles are different from what they were when we first published our work. Each member is responsible for guiding learning as the group uses the before-, during-, and after-reading strategies. Cue cards prompt students as they take the lead in their designated roles. The goal is for the strategies to guide students in engaging in meaningful discussions about the content they are learning. Although group discussions and shared ideas are important aspects of CSR group work, individual accountability is also essential. For each strategy, students think about and record individual responses in CSR learning logs. This process provides wait time so that all students are prepared to share their ideas with one another. Group discussions also provide comprehensible input, which is particularly important for English language learners when gleaning meaning from content. The learning logs also become an important source of information for teacher feedback as well as a springboard for follow-up activities.

A RESEARCH-BASED PROGRAM

CSR was developed with and for teachers. Over the years, we have collaborated with numerous teachers to help them implement CSR in their classrooms and to learn from them as they have tried CSR with their students and made adjustments to make it more feasible and effective. We have learned much from teachers, including (but not limited to) Tiffany Bart, Juan Cabrera, and Lucille Sullivan. We include some of their ideas in the pages of this book. To learn more about the evolution of CSR and the research base behind it, consult Appendix B.

CSR is not a curriculum in a box, but rather a flexible set of strategies used by students working collaboratively, guided by their teachers. CSR can be used in science, social studies, reading intervention, and language arts classes. CSR helps students to access content, to improve their understanding, and to be more thoughtful, purposive readers.

Part I

Getting to Know Collaborative Strategic Reading

CHAPTER 1

How CSR Works

> " *Of probably all of the things I have done, with pre-AP or the differentiation or the other things the district has thrown at me in seven years, this is probably the only one I will keep and I'm hard to convince. I'm hard to convince and this one has.* "
>
> —MIDDLE SCHOOL LANGUAGE ARTS TEACHER

> " *I think CSR is wonderful. It's an excellent program. It's practical; it focuses kids; it has all the elements in reading that they need and it's lifelong.* "
>
> —MIDDLE SCHOOL READING INTERVENTION TEACHER

> " *CSR is an excellent technique for teaching students reading comprehension and building vocabulary and also working together cooperatively. I think it is wonderful. We have been using it with the science text and it's turned out beautifully.* "
>
> —FIFTH-GRADE TEACHER

In this chapter, we describe CSR. We discuss each of the strategies and provide examples of students working together in small groups. CSR strategies occur before, during, and after reading (see Figure 1.1).

Before Reading: Preview

Students preview the entire passage before they read each section. The goals of previewing are (1) for students to learn as much about the passage as they can in a brief period of time (two to three minutes), (2) to activate their background knowledge about

FIGURE 1.1. CSR Comprehension Strategies

Reprinted with permission from the Meadows Center for Preventing Educational Risk (2009). *CSR strategies*. Austin, TX: Janette Klingner and Sharon Vaughn.

the topic, and (3) to make predictions about what they will learn. Previewing serves to motivate students' interest in the topic and to engage them in active reading from the onset. Preview also provides opportunities to help students develop background knowledge about the reading, and build vocabulary and concepts to enhance their understanding of the passage.

When students preview before reading, they should look at the following:

- The passage's title
- Any headings
- Words that are bolded or underlined
- Any pictures, tables, graphs, and other key information

This will help them do two things:

- Brainstorm what they already know about the topic
- Predict what they will learn about the topic

The teacher leads the preview portion of CSR. In previous versions of CSR,[1] students conducted a student-guided preview while working together in their small groups. Over the years, we have found that students do not always have sufficient background knowledge about a topic or sufficiently understand how the topic of the day's reading connects with other lessons. This is especially true when students begin a new unit of study. Therefore, we now ask teachers to facilitate the Preview. That way, the teacher can preteach a few key vocabulary words; provide a short video clip, pictures, chart, or diagram to help build background knowledge about the topic of the passage; and give students feedback on their brainstorms and predictions, helping them to make connections. While leading the Preview, the teacher asks students to write their brainstorm statements and predictions in their learning logs and to share with one another (either with a partner or in small groups) (see Figure 1.2).

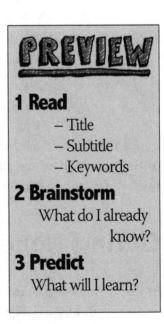

FIGURE 1.2. The Preview Process

In the following example, students from an eighth-grade language arts class are sharing their predictions while reading "The Odyssey":

Gabrielle:	Do you guys have what you think might happen today?
Nate:	I have mine.
Cassidy:	Yes, me too, I have it.
James:	Mmm, I don't know . . .
Gabrielle:	Well, I thought that we might learn about his journey from Achilles, because I looked ahead and I got to see the picture.
Cassidy:	Mine is sort of like yours. I said that I think he [Ulysses] is going to be learning about, um, the land of the dead, because that is obviously the title, and that can help, so that's what I think it's about.

In the next example, seventh-graders are sharing their predictions about an article that describes the melting of the polar ice cap. The teacher has already conducted a whole-class Preview and has asked students to share their predictions. David is an English language learner (ELL) with learning disabilities who reads at about a second-grade level.

Cinthia:	Okay, I think that I might learn what is happening in the North Pole and the effects of the ice melting and what it can do and what can happen.
David:	Good job, Cinthia.
Cinthia:	Thank you.
Laura:	I might learn about the topic, how to help the environment and how to keep the ice, keep it safe. David?
David:	I think I'm gonna learn how to find out what the climate is and how it is changing.
Katy:	Okay, I put that I think that we will learn about how to prevent this and what we can do about it.

Although David might not be able to read every word in the passage, he was able to glean enough about the passage from previewing it and from hearing his peers' predictions to come up with his own prediction.

During Reading: Click and Clunk

Students Click and Clunk while reading each section of the passage. One section of a passage typically consists of one to three paragraphs. Sometimes sections of text in a textbook are set off by subheadings that make it easy to separate them. At other times, the teacher decides where to separate the passage. Three sections of text for one day's reading works well. Students learn to think about what they are reading and to determine if there is a word or concept that they do not understand. They learn to refer to this as a *clunk*. Students are then asked to underline or write down their clunks.

The goal of teaching students about Click and Clunk is to get them to monitor their understanding while they read and to determine whether they have "meaning" breakdowns. In other words, Click and Clunk helps students develop the metacognitive awareness that is so important for successful reading.

Many students with reading difficulties fail to adequately monitor their understanding while they are reading. Click and Clunk is designed to serve as a trigger for monitoring their understanding. Clicks refer to portions of the text that make sense to the reader: *click, click, click*—comprehension clicks into place as the reader proceeds smoothly through the text. When students come to a word, concept, or idea that does not make sense, they are taught to think of that as a

CLICK and CLUNK

1 Look for Clunks.
   Find words or ideas I don't understand.
2 Use fix-up strategies.
   –Reread sentence with clunk.
   –Reread sentence before and after clunk.
   –Look for prefix, suffix, and root word.
   –Look for cognate.

FIGURE 1.3. The Click and Clunk Process

clunk, a bump in the road where comprehension breaks down. Initially, the teacher asks, "Is everything clicking? Who has clunks about the section we just read?" Students know that they will be asked this question and are alert to identify clunks during reading. Over time, students take on the responsibility for identifying their own clunks. See Figure 1.3 for a summary of Click and Clunk.

Learning to identify clunks is important. But what do students do after they determine that there is a word or concept they do not know? Students use fix-up strategies to figure out the meaning of clunks. The first two fix-up strategies rely on context clues, or "reading around" the word or words in question. The second two fix-up strategies require looking within the word. One relies on studying word parts (i.e., morphology) and the other asks students to consider if there are cognates in another language that can help. Here are the four strategies to fix up a clunk:

- *Fix-up strategy one:* Reread the sentence with the clunk and look for key ideas to help you figure out the word. Think about what makes sense.

- *Fix-up strategy two:* Reread the sentence with the clunk and the sentences before or after the clunk looking for clues.

- *Fix-up strategy three:* Break the word apart and look for a prefix, suffix, or a root word.

- *Fix-up strategy four:* Look for a cognate that makes sense.

After reading a section of text, the Leader in a CSR group asks everyone to write down any clunks they have. Then the Leader asks, "Clunk Expert, please help us out." The Clunk Expert then asks if anyone in the group knows the meaning of the clunk. If that is the case, the student who knows the meaning of the word or concept explains it and makes sure everyone understands. Before moving on, students reread the sentence with the clunk to make sure the definition makes sense. If no one in the group can explain the meaning of the clunk, then the Clunk Expert guides the group through the application of the fix-up strategies as they try to solve the clunk. If they are still stuck, the Leader asks for the teacher's assistance.

In the following example, students in a seventh-grade class are helping one another figure out the meaning of a clunk, *noxious*. Two of the students are struggling readers (Julie and Michael) and two are average to high achievers (Cinthia and Raul). Note that it was an average to high achiever who came up with the clunk.

Cinthia:	Noxious.
Julie:	Do you know; does anyone know what this clunk means?
Michael:	What's your clunk?
Cinthia:	Noxious.
Raul:	Isn't it a feeling you get when like . . .
Cinthia:	That's nauseous (laughing).
Raul:	Oh.
Cinthia:	Nauseous is, like, when you want to throw up.
Michael:	It's, like, a chemical—
Julie:	—a chemical that kills.
Raul:	OK, let's reread the sentence, come on. "Cotton plants, for instance, are often smothered with *noxious* chemicals to keep away bugs and weeds." Noxious.
Julie:	So, it kills, so it's a chemical.
Cinthia:	So, it's like something bad if it kills the bugs and weeds.
Julie:	It's something that kills—
Raul:	—bad for the environment.
Michael:	Yeah.
Cinthia:	It's something that's not good.
Michael:	It's something that kills.
Raul:	It's like toxic.

The following example is from a fifth-grade class. Students are using CSR while reading their science textbook. Diana is the Leader and Greg is the Clunk Expert. Pablo is an ELL with learning disabilities. Greg offers procedural and conceptual explanations and checks for understanding:

Diana:	Click and Clunk?
Pablo:	Calcium.
Greg:	Try to read sentences in the back and in the front to try to get a clue. Think if you see any sentences in the back or in the front that can help you. Did you get anything?
Pablo:	No.
Greg:	OK, now I do, I get something. It is a tiny crystal-like mineral. Do you know what a mineral is?
Pablo:	Yeah.
Greg:	What is it?
Pablo:	It's like a kind of vitamin.
Greg:	OK, calcium is a type of element that there is in the bones. And, the bones need that. Calcium helps the bones in order to make them strong. Do you now understand what calcium is?
Pablo:	Yes.
Greg:	What is it again, one more time?
Pablo:	It is a type of element that helps the bones grow.
Greg:	OK, good.

During Reading: Get the Gist

In CSR, students learn to use two strategies while they read, Click and Clunk and Get the Gist. The previous section described how teachers can help students determine clunks and then use fix-up strategies to better understand these clunks. In this section, we describe how teachers can use Get the Gist with their students to facilitate their ability to determine the main idea of a text and to write or state the main idea in their own words.

> Students get the gist by identifying the most important idea in a section of text (usually about two paragraphs). When students can restate in their own words the most important information about what they read, it is a very good indicator of reading comprehension.

In addition to improving understanding, learning to effectively Get the Gist of targeted text promotes students' memory for what they have learned. Also, getting the gist across multiple paragraphs in a section of text requires higher-level thinking. Students must synthesize information, decide what is more important, and determine which details to leave out (see Figure 1.4).

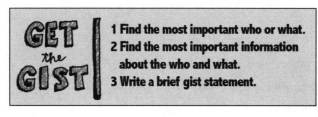

FIGURE 1.4. The Get the Gist Process

While working in their small groups, students Get the Gist after reading a section of text, right after they have finished figuring out their clunks. The Leader asks the Gist Expert to take charge. The Gist Expert then asks everyone in the group to name the topic, or, in other words, the most important who or what the section of text is about. Once students agree on the topic, then the Gist Expert asks all in the group to write their own gists in their learning logs. Once students have had time to do this, the Gist Expert asks everyone to share. Students then evaluate each others' gists, pointing out when they think a gist includes details or leaves out an important idea. The goal of CSR at this point is for students to engage in a rich content-focused discussion about the important ideas in the text they are reading.

In the following example, the same seventh-graders we heard from previously are now getting the gist. Note how Raul questions Julie about her gist, pointing out that she left out some important information (i.e., "the bad part").

Julie: OK, go ahead, Cinthia.

Cinthia: Many of the companies make clothes out of chemicals that hurt the earth, but earth-friendly fabrics help the earth.

Julie: OK, mine was, Clothes and shoes involves chemicals and energy but now involves corn sugar.

Pause (three seconds)

Julie: So let's just keep going.

Raul: No, but the bad part. This was the thing they were trying to do; this was the bad part. We didn't quite get the bad part.

Julie: What do you mean, the bad part?

Raul: *(pointing to the text)* They're using synthetic fibers from petroleum *(pointing to the words in the passage and tapping them)* and they get it from the ground, processing it from the oil . . .

Cinthia: Well, if you did all that, it wouldn't fit.

Julie: Yeah, and I did kinda write it cause I wrote that clothes and shoes involves harsh chemicals and energy, but now they are trying to make it out of corn sugar—

Raul: —with corn sugar.

Julie: Yeah, now they're trying to make it, um, to *(reading)* "overcome this reliance, some companies have experimented with creating materials from substances such as corn sugar."

Cinthia: 'Cause if you put all those things that they make it out of, it will like take—

Julie: —take too long.

Cinthia:	Yeah.
Julie:	That's why I just wrote the chemicals. OK, who wants to read the third section?

The next example is from a fifth-grade class.

Mario:	What is the most important idea we have learned about the topic so far? José?
José:	That when drugs are abused, drugs can be dangerous and very harmful.
Laura:	That when drugs are taken as directed, they can help.
José:	But, drugs can also be misused or used improperly.
Mario:	OK, but can we put those together?
Laura:	Drugs help when used properly but can be dangerous when misused.

After Reading: Wrap Up

Like the Preview stage, Wrap Up occurs only once and at the end of reading the assigned text. Wrap Up gives students the opportunity to think about the entire text and what they have learned. The goals are to improve students' knowledge, understanding, and memory of what they have just finished reading. Wrap Up has two parts. First, students formulate teacherlike questions about the important ideas in the text. They take turns asking and answering these questions in their small groups. To help them generate different types of questions, students learn three types of question-answer relationships (QAR). (QAR is a tool for helping students understand that they need to consider information in the text as well as their background knowledge when generating and answering questions):[2]

- *Right There*, for which the answer is in one place in the text

- *Think and Search*, for which the answer can be found in multiple places in the text and must be synthesized

- *Author and You*, for which some of the information needed to answer the question is in the text and other information is from the reader's background knowledge

Students might also use question stems, such as the following:

- How were _____ and _____ the same? How were they different?
- What do you think would happen if _____?
- What do you think caused _____ to happen?
- What other solution can you think of for the problem of _____?
- What might have prevented the problem of _____ from happening?
- What are the strengths (or weaknesses) of _____?

These question stems can be helpful for all students and especially for ELLs.

1 Question
– Right There
– Think and Search
– Author and You
2 Review
Identify the
most important
information.

FIGURE 1.5. The Wrap Up Process

Next, as the final step in their small groups, students review the important ideas they have learned. They write down a few key ideas from the text, share them with peers, and justify why they think they are important (see Figure 1.5). To help them think about what was important, students review their learning logs, paying particular attention to the gist statements.

When it is time to Wrap Up, the Leader asks the Question Expert to guide the group in writing, answering, and discussing questions. The Question Expert might remind the group of the three question types. The Question Expert also makes sure that students answer their classmates' questions and agree on the response. The Leader then guides the Review of important information by asking all to write down the most important ideas they have learned and then asking who would like to share. Next we provide two examples, one of questioning and another of review.

In this first example, fifth-graders answer Tasha's question. Note that Tasha exaggerates a bit—ideally, this is something the teacher would pick up on and clarify.

Tasha: What might happen if your bones did not contain enough calcium?

Luis: They will break.

Tasha: OK, they will probably break. But can we add a little bit?

Rolando: Well, first of all, what is calcium? And then we can figure out what it says and how it helps the bones.

Luis: OK, calcium is something that keeps the bones healthy and stuff like that.

Erica: Tasha?

Tasha: If you don't have enough calcium the bones will rot and you will be dead. And, then after you die you know your bones decay and you turn into dust. Your bones will like decompose in your body which will destroy and corrupt. If it does not have enough calcium, then the bones will get weak and break.

Erica: OK, I would say the same thing because the bones without calcium are nothing.

Rolando: All right, well, we finished this.

Next, a group of seventh-graders review the most important ideas in a passage they read about the polar ice cap melting. Laura, Katy, and Cinthia all are average achieving, and David has learning disabilities and reads at about a second-grade level. Note that the teacher provides a brief minilesson about review statements. She did this because she had read the students' learning logs and noticed that they seemed to be writing more about interesting aspects than the most important points of readings.

Katy: Write one or more of the more important ideas in this text.

Teacher: When you're writing this part I want you to make sure that you're writing what's most important. Not what's most *interesting*, but what's most *important* in terms of understanding the information that's in the article. They presented a lot of different ideas and a lot of different information, but out of that I want you to be ready to tell your group why you think that's most important . . .

Laura: I put the temperatures are increasing so the perennial ice is melting and the perennial ice is the thick, thick ice, didn't it say that? It's like really, really thick.

Katy: I said the same thing as her and that the perennial ice is melting and that's worrying because the ice has frozen for many, many years.

Laura: And it's like really thick ice. Like it shouldn't be melting.

Cinthia: I put that temperatures are not the usual which has brought lots of damage like the annual ice. Which is like vulnerable 'cause that's the ice that's been there, too.

Katy: Are you finished, David?

David: Yeah, I put that the temperatures are increasing and causing the thick ice to melt.

Katy: That's mostly what we all wrote.

Cinthia: Yeah.

Katy: So it is a very important thing that it said in the article.

Cinthia: 'Cause it could do a lot of damage to us.

Katy: Mmm hmm. And that's all. But that's 65 percent. That's really big to me 'cause that just happened in a year imagine what can happen in one other year, three years it could all be gone—

Laura: —be gone.

Cinthia: Yeah, it says that unusual cold has raised hopes, so maybe we'll recover it, but maybe not.

Laura: 'Cause like—

Cinthia: —Maybe there won't be a chance.

David: A chance, yeah.

Laura: 'Cause maybe it will start to break again and maybe it will be bigger, like 75 percent next year. 'Cause this was 2008, 65 percent, and now we're 2009 so—

Katy: How much damage happened already?

Cinthia: We don't know that, and we don't know that we're causing this.

Whole-Class Wrap Up and Follow-Up Activities

Once students have finished generating questions and reviewing what they have learned in their CSR groups, the teacher leads a quick, whole-class Wrap Up to emphasize important information and help students make connections with other lessons and the big ideas or "essential questions" the class is focusing on. The teacher may also clarify misunderstandings noticed while students were working in small groups and engage students in higher-level thinking activities using the information they have learned. This whole-class Wrap Up might be done very quickly at the end of the period before students leave as a way to bring closure to the lesson. Or it might be much more involved and include follow-up activities.

Follow-up activities can vary depending on the goals of the class, the age and needs of the students, and the focus of the class. Tiffany Bart used a Numbered Heads Together[3] activity in her diverse fifth-grade classroom using questions students had generated in their groups. Students first numbered off. Mrs. Bart asked a question, and then students wrote their answers and discussed them in their groups, putting their heads together to make sure everyone in the group knew the answer to the question. Then Mrs. Bart rolled two dice; one number indicated which group should respond and the second number represented which student in the group to call on. Mrs. Royal kept score to make the activity more like a game. Students enjoyed this activity and always were very highly engaged when they played.

Another activity Mrs. Bart's students loved was "Jeopardy," again using questions they had generated. Right-There questions were worth ten points each, Think-and-Search questions were worth twenty points, and Author-and-You questions were worth the most points. Mrs. Bart also sometimes had groups send their best question to a neighboring group to answer in a version of "Send a Problem."[4]

Not all of Mrs. Bart's follow-up activities involved questions, though. She also had students complete a variety of tasks to reinforce vocabulary, including putting clunks and their definitions on a word wall and creating clunk books as homework. Sometimes students checked the accuracy of the definitions they had come up with using fix-up strategies in their groups. They liked to play games with their clunks, such as "Clunk Concentration," which involved matching clunk words and their definitions.

Teachers might also provide additional instruction in prefixes, root words, suffixes, and cognates. Students might develop clunk graphic and semantic organizers or engage in other activities to reinforce new vocabulary learning. They could also write longer summaries of multiple passages they have read on the same topic.

To Sum Up

When it is up and running and working as it should, CSR brings out the best in everyone involved. Teachers are able to circulate around the classroom and provide support on an as-needed basis. They have the time to provide individual assistance to students who are in need or feedback, to an entire small group, or to the whole class. Students are all actively involved in learning and supporting one another.

Part II

Teaching CSR in the Classroom

CHAPTER 2

Teaching the CSR Strategies to Students

> "It's a great way to get all kids involved. Because I have kids who won't do anything when you are doing a regular lesson but all of a sudden [in CSR], they are engaged and doing it."
>
> —MIDDLE SCHOOL LANGUAGE ARTS TEACHER

> "It sort of runs itself, you know, and that's wonderful! I look forward to CSR days. I just kind of help facilitate their learning and it's not direct instruction anymore. And it's so nice getting to that point."
>
> —MIDDLE SCHOOL READING INTERVENTION TEACHER

> "CSR is great for kids with LD [learning disabilities] because they contribute to their groups and feel successful, and they get the help they need with their reading."
>
> —K-6 SPECIAL EDUCATION TEACHER

To get CSR effectively implemented in classrooms, teachers first teach students how to use each of the CSR strategies separately through whole-class instruction and practice with partners or in small groups. In this chapter, we provide a set of instructional guides with descriptions of teacher and student actions that may take place as teachers introduce each new strategy, model use, and provide students with guided and independent practice opportunities. If you are a teacher, these guides are ready for you to use in your classroom. If you are a professional development provider or an instructional coach, they may serve as handouts during your presentations or coaching sessions. These lesson instructional guides are not meant to be used as a script but rather as models.

CSR strategies are each taught separately so that students have time to learn and practice them. Typically the Preview strategy is taught first, followed by Click and Clunk and Get the Gist, and then Wrap Up. After each strategy is taught, it should be practiced during lessons on new strategies. In this way, isolated introduction of strategies is

---

EXHIBIT 2.1. Introducing the CSR Strategies

1. Introduce each strategy one at a time. Use the lesson instructional outlines.

2. Allow multiple opportunities for students to practice with the class and then in small groups, using CSR roles.

3. When students have learned all the strategies, move into cooperative learning groups of about four students.
   - Groups are student-led. Students use peers to support learning.
   - The teacher's role is to provide focused feedback and to support high-level discussions, strategy use, and content learning.

4. Monitor progress and reteach as needed.

---

avoided. Instead, students consistently practice and learn new skills over time until they integrate all four strategies into their text reading.

Although there are many ways to introduce the strategies, teachers often find it helpful to use a common scaffolding procedure (see Exhibit 2.1). For each strategy, the teacher first provides direct instruction and models how to use the strategy. Next, students are provided opportunities to practice the strategy on their own and with other students. Once students are familiar with a strategy, they can practice it in cooperative groups, adding on strategies as they are learned.

Because CSR is an organizing framework for engaging students in cognitively challenging tasks during the reading process rather than a set curriculum, it is up to you to choose the most appropriate text for your students as you teach CSR. Selections are from a passage we wrote called "Ben Franklin and Electricity," which is used throughout this chapter for illustration purposes.[1]

During CSR instruction and practice, students should use a CSR learning log. The log provides space for students to record their work before, during, and after reading and is useful for several purposes:

- Students can later use CSR learning logs to prepare for tests, writing assignments, and class discussions.

- As a source of accountability, logs provide a record of completion and quality of work.

- Teachers can refer to logs during CSR lessons to inform the type of feedback they provide students to improve their comprehension of text.

- Teachers can review logs to determine the content of subsequent instruction that targets areas of continued academic need.

- Many teachers grade the CSR learning logs.

Teachers have designed many forms of the log since it was first introduced in 1998. Samples of learning logs are provided throughout this chapter. (See Appendix A for additional versions and other CSR classroom materials.)

Before Reading: Preview

Teach students to preview a passage so that they can get a sense for what it will be about and to activate background knowledge. When teaching students to Preview, it is helpful to connect them to what a movie preview does. Ask students how many of them have seen a movie preview, what they learned from the preview, and what they might think about when watching a preview:

- Do you learn who is going to be in the movie?
- Do you learn during what historical period the movie will take place?
- Do you learn whether or not you might like the movie?
- Do you think about what the movie reminds you of, perhaps another movie you have seen?
- Do you have questions about what more you would like to know about the movie?

Let students know that we can find out similar information when we preview what we read. We learn who or what the text is about and where and when it occurs. We make connections with what we already know. We can also make predictions about what will happen or what we will learn when we read.

It helps students if we demonstrate how to preview. Here is an example of how one teacher modeled previewing for her students. Ms. Chou provided all of her students with a brief text to read (approximately six paragraphs). She told them, "I am going to show you the kinds of skills you need to use when you preview. First, I look at the title and any pictures and ask myself if I can imagine what it is going to be about. Second, I look for headings, key words in italics or bold, and think about what they tell me about the reading. Next, I skim the first paragraph and the last paragraph and think about what I already know about the topic and how this connects. Then I am ready to make a prediction about what I'm going to learn about when I read." She gave her students one and a half minutes to write down everything they already know about a topic, and then about one minute to share their responses with a partner or groupmates. She then provided another one and a half minutes for students to write down predictions of what they might learn, followed by one minute to share with one another.

You may teach students the Preview strategy from the beginning of the school year and have them use it before they read aloud or silently. Like the other CSR strategies, you may apply it across the curriculum. By using Preview in different subject areas, students learn to internalize the strategies and transfer them across situations. They will also have had opportunities to watch you model and apply the strategy with the class as a whole, making its implementation in small groups easier.

LESSON INSTRUCTIONAL GUIDE: Preview

➔ *Time:* About seven minutes

➔ *When:* Before reading text passage

➔ *How:* Preview should always be teacher led. Students are active participants in the Preview routine.

➔ *Purpose:* The purpose of the Preview is to introduce the topic, access and build background knowledge, and set a purpose for reading.

1. Introduce the Topic

2. Preteach Key Proper Nouns and Vocabulary

TEACHER ACTION	STUDENT ACTION
Write key proper nouns and vocabulary on display board.	Listen attentively.
Tell students the word and a short, student-friendly definition and show a visual representation (e.g., teacher may show a picture of Ben Franklin holding a kite with a key on it during a lightning storm).	Students may repeat the word or definition to the teacher or a peer.
Key vocabulary from "Ben Franklin":	
• *Hypothesis* • *Conductor*	

3. Preview the Text

TEACHER ACTION	STUDENT ACTION
Ask students why it is important to preview text (tell them if they do not generate a reason): • So students can learn as much as possible about the passage in a short time This is a good time to use the movie preview analogy: *When you go to the movies, how many of you watch the previews? What happens during a preview? You learn about the movie. Let's think about what we learn in the one-minute preview.* • *Do we learn who is in the movie?* • *Do we learn when and where the movie takes place?* *We can also make some predictions about what will happen in the movie—what some of the key events might be. We can do some of these same things during a Preview. We can* • *Learn about who or what the text is about* • *Where and when the reading occurs* • *Make predictions about what will happen or what we will learn*	Students might • Share their responses with a partner • Answer questions as part of a whole-class discussion Students may record the steps in a notebook for future reference. Otherwise, they should listen attentively. Students should follow along in the text providing responses to teacher prompts and questions.

TEACHER ACTION	STUDENT ACTION
Tell students the three steps for previewing text: • Read the title. • Read the subheadings and think about how they relate to the topic. • Look at pictures, charts, and information boxes and think about how they relate to the topic. Conduct a think-aloud as you guide students through these three steps.	

4. Brainstorm What Is Known About the Topic (Access and Build Background Knowledge)

TEACHER ACTION	STUDENT ACTION
Write (so that students can see) one to two statements of what you already know about the topic. Ask students to brainstorm what they already know about the topic. Remind them that this information can be something they have already learned in school or perhaps at home, on TV, in a book, or from someone else. *Write two to three things you already know about Benjamin Franklin.* Ask students to share their ideas with a partner or in small groups and then ask a few students to share with the entire class. If students' brainstorms seem unrelated to the topic, try to figure out how the students see a connection and clarify any misunderstandings.	Listen attentively and read what the teacher writes. Record two to three statements on their learning log. Students might • Share their responses with a partner or in small groups • Share their responses as part of a whole-class discussion

Tips for accessing and building background knowledge:

- Sometimes students need prompts to make connections to what they already know. Ask them to think of something in their own lives that is similar to the content.

- Capitalize on the opportunity to build background knowledge through explanations, examples, and supplementary materials, such as pictures, charts, models, or even a short video clip.

5. Predict What Will Be Learned from the Topic

TEACHER ACTION	STUDENT ACTION
Teach students how to make good predictions. *There are three steps to making a good prediction:* • *Use clues from the text preview.* • *Make an educated guess about what you might learn.* • *Write one to two predictions of what you think the passage will be about.* Model for students each step in making a good prediction. *Watch and follow along as I make a prediction using our three steps.* Ask students to write their own predictions. *Now I want you to take another minute to predict what you will learn. Based on our Preview of the title, headings, and illustrations, write a list of one or two things you think you will learn about.* Ask students to share their ideas with a partner or in small groups and then ask a few students to share with the entire class. If students' predictions seem unrelated to the topic or too general, prompt them to look at the text again. Ask them to explain how they came up with their predictions.	Students might repeat to a partner the steps for making a good prediction. Listen attentively and read what the teacher writes. Record two to three predictions on their learning log. Students might • Share their responses with a partner or in small groups • Share their responses as part of a whole-class discussion

6. Set a Purpose for Reading

TEACHER ACTION	STUDENT ACTION
State (in one to two sentences) a purpose for reading that is related to the topic you stated at the beginning of the lesson and that incorporates students' predications. *Your predictions can guide your reading. Let me show you how. Some of you thought you'd learn more about who Ben Franklin was and what he discovered. So, today, as you read, I want you to think about these two questions:* • *Who was Ben Franklin?* *and* • *What did he discover about electricity?*	Students listen attentively.

During Reading: Click and Clunk

Teach students to monitor their comprehension while reading and to take steps to improve their understanding. Ms. Lang taught Click and Clunk this way: "When something clicks, you really understand it. It is something that you 'get' and you may even know more about it than what is provided in the text. For example, I was reading a newspaper article this morning about how to grow tomatoes. Well, the article really clicked for me because I've been growing tomatoes for fourteen years. I really understand what the author meant when she said you have to space young plants at least twelve inches apart. However, there were several clunks in the article for me. I did not know the terms 'organic matter' and 'cover crop.'"[2] Ms. Lang then proceeded to demonstrate for the students how she used the fix-up strategies to figure out what the words *organic matter* and *cover crop* meant in the article she was reading.

Ms. Lang modeled several times how she identified clunks in text she was reading and showed the students how to use the fix-up strategies by "thinking aloud" how she used them to repair her understanding of text. She then practiced identifying clunks by reading text aloud to the students and providing them with an opportunity to record any clunks they heard while she read. She then used the four fix-up strategies with students to build understanding of the clunks they identified. Initially using relatively brief segments of text (e.g., two to four paragraphs), Ms. Lang asked students to read and underline text and then to practice using fix-up strategies to see if they could learn more about the clunk. In Ms. Lang's class, students became "clunk detectors" throughout the day—thinking about words and ideas they did not understand and working alone or with partners to see if they could figure them out in different subject areas. As students learned to identify and resolve clunks using the fix-up strategies with relatively brief segments of text and with teacher instruction and feedback, students then progressed to using Click and Clunk while working on their own in small groups.

Mrs. Sullivan also encouraged her students to Click and Clunk throughout the day. She suggested that students identify clunks in the books or other materials they read at home. When students came to school, she would often start the day with, "Does anyone have any clunks?" In this way, students learned to be mindful of words and ideas they read or heard inside and outside of school. Teaching students to be word conscious is an important way to expand their word and world knowledge.

LESSON INSTRUCTIONAL GUIDE: Click and Clunk

➤ *Time:* When students identify a clunk, they should spend approximately one minute applying the fix-up strategies to repair meaning. Two to three clunks per section of text in a group is about right.

➤ *When:* During reading

➤ *How:* During teacher-led modeling and guided practice, students are highly engaged in contributing to class work and practice. Once students master the fix-up strategies, they may use them during independent reading or group work time.

➜ *Purpose:* The purpose of the Click and Clunk strategy is to recognize when a passage makes sense (clicks), when there are breakdowns in understanding (clunks), and to use fix-up strategies to repair breakdowns.

1. Tell Students About the Click and Clunk Strategy

What is it?

Why use it?

TEACHER ACTION	STUDENT ACTION
Provide an analogy for understandings and breakdowns in comprehension while reading text.	Listen attentively and respond to teacher prompts and questions.
Example: "Driving a car" analogy	
When I think of the Click and Clunk strategy, I think of driving a car. When you drive and everything moves smoothly, you click along, but when you hit a pothole, you CLUNK—hit it. It disrupts your smooth driving. You can think about clicks and clunks when you're reading, too.	
Example: "Skateboard" analogy	
When I think of the Click and Clunk strategy, I think of a skateboard. When you are riding and everything moves smoothly, you click along, but when you try to do a trick and can't quite do it, CLUNK—you need to stop and try again or try something different. You can think about Click and Clunk when you're reading, too.	
Most of the time, when you're reading, you understand the words . . . you CLICK right along.	
But, sometimes you—CLUNK!—get stuck on a word or phrase that you do not understand.	
Tell how the Click and Clunk strategy will help.	
Identifying clunks and figuring out what they mean will help you understand what you read without using a computer or dictionary. I am going to show you how to fix up your clunks today.	

2. Overview of How to Use the Click and Clunk Strategy

TEACHER ACTION	STUDENT ACTION
Tell the steps of the Click and Clunk strategy.	Listen attentively and respond to teacher prompts and questions.
• *Identify clunks and write them in your learning log.*	
• *Use fix-up strategies to figure out the meaning of the clunks.*	
• *Write a brief definition or explanation in your learning log.*	
Tell students that over the next few days, they will learn how to use four different fix-up strategies to figure out the meanings of their clunks.	

As described in Chapter One, here are the four fix-up strategies to employ during Click and Clunk:

Fix-up strategy one: Reread the sentence with the clunk and look for key ideas to help you figure out the word. Think about what makes sense.

Fix-up strategy two: Reread the sentence with the clunk and the sentences before or after the clunk looking for clues.

Fix-up strategy three: Break the word apart and look for a prefix, suffix, or a root word.

Fix-up strategy four: Look for a cognate that makes sense.

3. Model the Click and Clunk Strategy (Fix-Up Strategies One and Two)

We suggest modeling fix-up strategies one and two during one class period followed by one to two days of guided practice (you may spend a greater or fewer number of days in the guided practice phase depending on your students' ability to use the fix-up strategies) until they gain mastery of the fix-up strategies. Exhibit 2.2 provides an example of a fix-up strategy practice sheet. Additional practice sheets may be created for subsequent class periods or for homework.

Use a progress monitoring measure to evaluate students' mastery of fix-up strategies one and two (see Chapter Four for more information about using student data to make instructional decisions). After a majority of students have mastered using fix-up strategies one and two, model and practice fix-up strategies three and four.

EXHIBIT 2.2. Fix-Up Strategies One and Two Example

Strategy one: Reread the sentence with the clunk and look for key ideas to help you figure out the word. Think about what makes sense.

Strategy two: Reread the sentences before and after the clunk, looking for clues.

Read the sentence and use fix-up strategy one or two to figure out the meaning of the underlined clunk. Write the definition of the clunk on the line below and circle which fix-up strategy you used.

1. The whale's <u>fluke</u>, or tail, has a notch down the middle.

   Fluke: _____ 1 2

2. A soft breeze can lift a leaf and make it dance. A <u>forceful</u> wind can lift a car and hurl it.

   Forceful: _____ 1 2

3. Have you ever seen what lightning can do when it strikes a building? It is so powerful that a strike can cause buildings and other structures to <u>erupt</u> in flames.

   Erupt: _____ 1 2

4. Benjamin Franklin helped <u>draft</u>, or write, the Constitution of the United States of America.

   Draft: _____ 1 2

TEACHER ACTION	STUDENT ACTION
Display fix-up strategies one and two. Read fix-up strategies one and two to students. Explain and model fix-up strategies one and two using Exhibit 2.2 as a basis. For example : *The whale's fluke, or tail, has a notch down the middle. My clunk is <u>fluke.</u> I'm not sure what that means. I will use fix-up strategy one: reread the sentence with the clunk and look for key ideas to help me figure out the clunk.* *The answer is right there in the sentence. It says that the whale's fluke is also its tail. So, fluke must mean "a whale's tail." I'll write that on my practice sheet.* *I used fix-up strategy one to figure out the meaning of my clunk, so I will circle "1" out to the side.* Continue modeling through the remainder of the practice sheet.	Students may read fix-up strategies one and two aloud. Follow along with the teacher model and complete practice sheet (such as Exhibit 2.2) with teacher guidance. When students are able to perform the strategy on their own, they should do so independently, with a partner, or in small groups.

4. Practice the Click and Clunk Strategy (Fix-Up Strategies One and Two)

TEACHER ACTION	STUDENT ACTION
Practice using fix-up strategies one and two using practice sheets similar to Exhibit 2.2 or use text coupled with a learning log. Students should follow the same procedure as in modeling whereby they figure out the meaning of their clunk and then identify the fix-up strategy used to figure out the meaning. Additional practice sheets may be created for subsequent class periods or for homework.	Follow along with the teacher model and complete practice sheet (such as Exhibit 2.2) with teacher guidance. When students are able to perform the strategy on their own, they should do so independently, with a partner, or in small groups.

5. Model the Click and Clunk Strategy (Fix-Up Strategies Three and Four)

Note: Fix-up strategy three relies on morphology (word parts that carry meaning). In other words, students look within the word (rather than around the word, as they do with fix-up strategies one and two). If your students are not familiar with prefixes, suffixes, and root words, you may need to conduct minilessons to teach some affixes before your students can successfully use fix-up strategy three.

TEACHER ACTION	STUDENT ACTION
Display fix-up strategies three and four. Read fix-up strategies three and four to students. Explain and model fix-up strategy three using words in isolation.	Read fix-up strategies three and four.

TEACHER ACTION	STUDENT ACTION
For example: *With fix-up strategies three and four, you examine the parts of the clunk itself. Let's start with fix-up strategy three.* Write the following words on the board or use a document camera and color code, highlight, or underline each word part, explaining to students how the affixes adjust the meaning of the root word: remake, walked, predawn, oversleep *Sometimes, you can figure out what a word means by recognizing its parts. For example, in the word* oversleep, *you probably recognize two words you know:* over *and* sleep. *In this case,* over *is a prefix that means "too much." So if you oversleep, you sleep too much, or sleep past the time you were supposed to get up.* Explain and model fix-up strategy four using words in isolation. *In fix-up strategy four, you look for a clunk's cognate. A cognate is a word in another language similar to the English word.* *English and Spanish have many cognates; cognates can help you make connections to what you already know.* Display examples of cognates where meaning transfers and also false cognates where meaning does not transfer. Discuss these with students. *Cognates can help you to figure out clunks, but be careful. There are a few words that look very similar in different languages but do not mean the same thing.* Read through the list of false cognates with students (see Exhibit 2.3). Ask students whether they can think of other false cognates and add them to the list. Model fix-up strategies three and four using words in context (see Exhibit 2.4).	Follow along with the teacher model and practice using fix-up strategy three with isolated words.

EXHIBIT 2.3. Cognates and False Cognates

EXAMPLES OF COGNATES

ENGLISH	SPANISH	DEFINITION
capital	*capital*	A city or town in which government leaders and others meet and work
communication	*comunicación*	Sharing ideas with others
community	*comunidad*	A place where people live and work near each other
desert	*desierto*	A dry place with very little rainfall
invention	*invención*	Something that has been created for the first time
island	*isla*	Land that has water all around it

(Continued)

EXAMPLES OF FALSE COGNATES

ENGLISH	SPANISH
globe	*globo* (balloon)
pie	*pie* (foot)
rope	*ropa* (clothes)
soap	*sopa* (soup or pasta)
large	*largo* (long)
exit	*éxito* (success)
embarrassed	*embarazada* (pregnant)

EXHIBIT 2.4. Fix-Up Strategies Three and Four Example

Strategy three: Look for a root word, prefix, or suffix in the word that might help.

Strategy four: Look for a cognate that makes sense.

Read the sentence and use fix-up strategy three or four to figure out the meaning of the underlined clunk. Write the definition of the clunk on the line below and circle which fix-up strategy you used.

1. After waiting for some time with the flying kite and seeing no signs of electricity, Franklin became <u>dispirited</u> and decided to go home.
   Dispirited: _____ 3 4

2. Taking the <u>upright</u> strands as a sign of an electrical current, Franklin extended his knuckle on the back of his hand out to the key and received an electric shock.
   Upright: _____ 3 4

3. Franklin's <u>investigation</u> with the kite and storm confirmed his hypothesis that lightning was made of electricity.
   Investigation: _____ 3 4

6. Practice the Click and Clunk Strategy (Fix-Up Strategies Three and Four)

TEACHER ACTION	STUDENT ACTION
Practice using fix-up strategies with longer passages similar in length to that found in Exhibit 2.5 or use text coupled with a learning log. Additional practice sheets may be created for subsequent class periods or for homework.	Follow along with the teacher model and complete practice sheets (such as Exhibits 2.4 and 2.5) with teacher guidance. When students are able to perform the strategy on their own, they should do so independently, with a partner, or in small groups.

EXHIBIT 2.5. Fix-Up Strategies Example

Name _____   Date _____

Today's Topic _____

Several possible clunks are underlined in the passage below. Write each clunk on the line below and use your fix-up strategies to identify the clunk's meaning. Write a short definition in the space to the right of your clunk. Circle the number corresponding to the fix-up strategy you used.

Ben <u>hypothesized</u>, or proposed, that lightning was a stream of electricity created in the clouds during a storm. In 1752, he <u>formulated</u> an experiment to test his idea. He planned to use a kite and metal key to direct the <u>flow</u> of electricity from clouds to the ground. If he could show <u>conduction</u> of the electrical stream through these materials, then he could prove that lightning was made of electricity.

CLUNKS	FIX-UP STRATEGIES	
_____ =	_____	1 2 3 4
_____ =	_____	1 2 3 4
_____ =	_____	1 2 3 4
_____ =	_____	1 2 3 4

During Reading: Get the Gist

The most common way to get the main idea in a section of text is taught in non–CSR classes. Teachers ask students to read a passage and to underline key ideas and then to tell them the main idea. For many students, especially those who have the most difficulty identifying main ideas, this exercise becomes a rote method of underlining the first or last sentence and then restating it to the teacher. Unfortunately, this method does not help students actually derive the main idea nor does it help them remember it by putting it in their own words.

We suggest teaching students to Get the Gist by the following:

- Identify whether the paragraphs were mostly about a person, place, or thing and write it down.

- Identify two or three important points about the most important person, place, or thing.

- Put this information together in about ten words or less and in complete sentence form.

The goal of this exercise is to get students to read for meaning and to think about the main who or what and what the most important elements of the section are. This provides a framework for students to then write a brief main idea statement that uses as few words as possible but still conveys the most meaning without unnecessary details. It is valuable for teachers to provide text to practice *getting* the gist that is supportive of *determining* the gist. We are all aware that some text does not readily allow for determining the gist because it is simply a list of facts without a clear unifying thread.

Michael Solis taught Get the Gist this way: He provided all students with a relatively brief passage (about six paragraphs) using information text related to something students were learning in social studies or science. He divided the six paragraphs into three sections with two paragraphs each. He directed students to read the first section (two paragraphs), thinking about whether the section is mainly about a person, place, or thing and to identify what it is. After students finished reading the paragraphs, he asked them to think about the passage they had just read and to write down the most important person, place, or thing in the section. Next, he asked students to share their ideas with a partner and to try to come up with an agreed-on topic. He then called on individual students to obtain their responses, asking other students whether they agreed and why. In one passage he used for this purpose, the most important who was Abraham Lincoln, and students readily agreed. He then asked students to write down several key points from the two paragraphs they had just read that would help them determine the gist and to discuss these points with their partners. Giving students five minutes to write and discuss their notes, he then called on various pairs of students to identify their key points. Writing their responses so they could be seen by the entire class, he asked other students to put a star by those key points they thought were essential, highlighting the difference between points that were of low and high importance in the text. Next, he asked students to take the key person the passage was about and the key ideas and put them together in their own words into a sentence using ten or fewer words to develop a gist. Allowing students a few minutes to complete this task, Mr. Solis then called on students to write their gists so that they would be visible to the class. He used these gists as opportunities to discuss what was "strong" and what could be "further developed" in each of the gists. Finally, he asked students to revise their gists to see if they could be improved. This iterative and visible process of discussing gists with the class as a whole provided opportunities to get feedback on developing gists so that members of the class improved in their understanding of key ideas within a passage, and how to synthesize them.

LESSON INSTRUCTIONAL GUIDE: Get the Gist

- *Time:* About three minutes per gist
- *When:* During reading
- *How:* During teacher-led modeling and guided practice, students are highly engaged in contributing to class work and practice. When students are more proficient with the Get the Gist strategy, they may use it during independent reading or group work time.
- *Purpose:* The purpose of the Get the Gist strategy is to determine the most important ideas about what is read.

1. Tell Students About the Get the Gist Strategy

What is it? Why use it?

TEACHER ACTION	STUDENT ACTION
Explain what Get the Gist is and why students should use the strategy. *Teachers in all of your classes ask you, "What was that section about?" On your tests, you see questions that ask, "What was the main idea?" Good readers stop every once in a while and ask themselves, "Do I understand what I'm reading?" Today, I'm going to teach you a strategy to use so that you can answer all of these questions. It is called* Get the Gist.	Listen attentively and respond to teacher prompts and questions.

2. Overview of How to Use the Get the Gist Strategy

TEACHER ACTION	STUDENT ACTION
Explain the steps of the Get the Gist strategy. *Get the Gist has three steps:* • *Identify the most important who or what in the passage.* • *Identify the most important information about the who or what.* • *Write a short, complete sentence containing the most important information.*	Listen attentively and respond to teacher prompts and questions.

3. Model the Get the Gist Strategy

TEACHER ACTION	STUDENT ACTION
Read a short paragraph.	Students either follow along while you read aloud or read the passage silently to themselves.
I am going to read the first paragraph of "Ben Franklin" aloud. Follow along while I read.	
Now that we've read the paragraph, let's identify the most important who or what. I think the most important who is Ben Franklin because most of the ideas in the paragraph are about Ben Franklin.	Students provide input as directed by the teacher.
Either think aloud or ask students to help you determine the most important information about the who or what.	
The second part of Get the Gist is to write the most important information about the who or what. Help me make a list of the most important information about Ben Franklin from this paragraph.	
Either think aloud or ask students to help you write a gist statement	
Now we need to write a gist statement. Remember, it needs to be a short sentence—about ten words long—that includes the most important ideas.	
Possible gist:	
Ben Franklin made important discoveries including preventing fire caused by lightning.	
See Exhibit 2.6 for an example of how students can fill in a Get the Gist log.	

4. Practice the Get the Gist Strategy

TEACHER ACTION	STUDENT ACTION
Continue modeling and engaging students in guided practice of Get the Gist until a majority of the class can write their own gist statement.	Students participate in guided practice activities.
Engage students in independent practice once they can use the strategy on their own.	When students are able to perform the strategy on their own, they should do so independently, with a partner, or in small groups.

EXHIBIT 2.6. Get the Gist Example

Name _____ Date _____

Mountain Bike

Many novice mountain bikers don't like to get going too fast when riding on a dirt trail. As a result, they are far more likely than experienced mountain bikers to rely heavily on their brakes. Although they may feel safer at a slower speed, they are actually at a greater risk for falling because a certain amount of momentum is needed to make small turns and adjustments. Whether you are riding uphill, downhill, or on a flat trail, the overuse of brakes makes it difficult to control your bicycle. Novice mountain bikers often learn the hard way that momentum is your friend.

Write a gist (short sentence of about ten words) for the passage above.

Gist: *Novice mountain bikers ride slowly although having some momentum is safer.*

After Reading: Wrap Up Question Generation

Asking students to generate questions about what they have read is a powerful comprehension strategy. Many teachers recognize that students have difficulty writing questions or that they write only very low-level detail questions. Tiffany Bart helped students learn to write questions starting with easier question stems and then provided them with more challenging ones. Initially, she taught students to ask questions that started with who, what, when, and where, recognizing that these questions usually related directly to the text and might be easier for them to develop.[3]

- Who was the inventor of the telephone?
- What happened after Madame Curie became famous?
- Where is Mount St. Helens?
- When did World War I begin?

After students demonstrated proficiency in easier questions, Mrs. Bart developed more challenging questions and assisted students in developing how and why questions in addition to more difficult questions starting with what, where, when, and how. Some sample question stems follow.

- How did what happened at the end differ from _____?
- How would you compare _____?
- What do you think would happen if _____?
- How do you think _____ might have been prevented?
- How would you interpret _____?
- Who else do you think could have influenced _____?
- What was the most important finding related to _____?

It may be useful to tell students to pretend they are teachers and to think of questions they would ask on a test to find out if their students really understood what they had read. Remember, learning to ask good questions is a great way to improve understanding of what you read, and it is also important that students know the answers to the questions that they ask. One way to help students learn whether their questions are well written and understandable is to answer them themselves, and to ask other students to answer the questions. If other students have difficulty answering a question because they do not understand what is being asked, it might mean it is not a good question and needs to be clarified.

Teach students to use question-answer relationships (QAR) when generating questions.[4] They ask Right-There questions about information that is stated explicitly in the passage in one place; Think-and-Search questions where the answer can be found in the passage but in more than one location; and Author-and-You questions that require an answer that draws from some information in the passage and also prior knowledge. Encourage students to ask questions that involve higher-level thinking skills rather than literal recall. Most questions can be improved with the addition of "Why do you think that?"

LESSON INSTRUCTIONAL GUIDE:
Question Generation—Right-There Questions

→ *Time:* Generating and answering questions takes about five minutes, one and a half to two minutes to write down questions and another three to three and a half minutes discussing them.

→ *When:* After reading

→ *How:* During teacher-led modeling and guided practice, students are highly engaged in contributing to class work and practice. Once students master writing questions, they may write independently or while working in their groups.

→ *Purpose:* The purpose of writing Right-There questions is to identify and remember key facts that are explicitly stated in the text. The purpose of writing Think-and-Search questions is to synthesize and remember key information from different sections of text that are critical to understanding the topic. Author-and-You questions help students to apply high-level inferencing skills and to make connections with the text.

1. Tell Students About Right-There Questions

What is it?

Why use it?

TEACHER ACTION	STUDENT ACTION
Explain what Right-There questions are and why students should learn to write them. *In every one of your classes, teachers ask you to remember what you read. You probably take tests and exams that contain questions about what you read. One way to remember information and to perform better on your tests is to write your own questions and answers. I will be teaching you how to write three types of questions to help you remember different types of information from your reading.* *The first type of question is called a* Right-There *question because the answer is "right there" in the text. These are usually facts.*	Listen attentively and respond to teacher prompts and questions.

2. Overview of How to Write Right-There Questions

TEACHER ACTION	STUDENT ACTION
Explain how to write a Right-There question. • Identify an important fact in the text that you want to remember. This will be the answer to your Right-There question. • Write a question that requires the answer you identified.	Listen attentively and respond to teacher prompts and questions.

3. Model How to Write Right-There Questions

TEACHER ACTION	STUDENT ACTION
Read a short paragraph. *I am going to read the first paragraph of the section entitled "Kite Experiment" aloud. Follow along while I read.* Either think aloud or ask students to help you determine an important fact they want or need to remember. *In this paragraph, I want to remember what Ben Franklin was trying to prove with his kite experiment. So, I'm going to write a Right-There question. Let's start the question with the word* what. *My question will read, "What did Ben Franklin want to prove with his kite experiment?"* *Now, I need an answer to my question. Let's reread the first sentence of the paragraph:* *"Ben hypothesized, or proposed, that lightning was a stream of electricity created in the clouds during a storm."* *There is my answer.* *I am going to write a complete sentence that reads:* *He wanted to prove that lightning is made of electricity.* Continue modeling if necessary.	Students either follow along while you read aloud or read the passage silently to themselves. Students provide input as directed by the teacher. Students write the question on their learning logs. Students may assist the teacher in locating the answer or writing the answer.

4. Practice How to Write Right-There Questions

TEACHER ACTION	STUDENT ACTION
Continue modeling and engaging students in guided practice of writing Right-There questions until a majority of the class can write and answer their own questions. *Now, you will write some Right-There questions on your own. Remember, you need to identify information you want or need to remember from the passage and write a question about that information.* *Write one Right-There question and answer from the section entitled "Kite Experiment." Be ready to share your question and answer with the class.* Exhibit 2.7 provides a sample learning log showing how students can write Right-There questions and answers. Monitor student work and provide feedback and guidance. As you monitor, note students who have written high-quality questions. Ask these students to share their questions with the class. Discuss why their questions are of high quality.	Students participate in guided practice activities. Students read passages and write (and answer) Right-There questions. They may work independently, with a partner, or in small groups.

EXHIBIT 2.7. Right-There Questions Example

Name _____ Date _____

A Right-There question is one that is answered with information found "right there" in the text. Read the following passage, then write two Right-There questions using information from the paragraph. Be sure to answer your questions as well.

> Have you ever seen what lightning can do when it strikes a building? It is so powerful that a strike can cause buildings and other structures to erupt in flames. During Ben Franklin's time, fires from lightning were a large concern for people. This is one reason he wanted to study lightning. Franklin was one of the greatest scientists of his time. Indeed, his work and experiments resulted in several important discoveries and inventions.

Write two Right-There questions (and answers) using information from the paragraph above.

What can lightning do when it strikes a building?
When lightning strikes a building, it can cause a fire.

What is one reason Ben Franklin wanted to study lightning?
Ben Franklin wanted to study lightning because lightning can cause fires.

LESSON INSTRUCTIONAL GUIDE:
Question Generation—Think-and-Search Questions

1. Tell Students About Think-and-Search Questions

What is it?

Why use it?

TEACHER ACTION	STUDENT ACTION
Explain what Think-and-Search questions are and why students should learn to write them. *You are in the process of learning how to write three types of questions to help you remember different types of information from your reading.* *The first type of question was called a Right-There question because the answer is "right there" in the text. These are usually facts.* *Today, you will be learning how to write Think-and-Search questions. These questions are more difficult to write. Sometimes, there is information scattered in different places in a passage. This information is related and you want to remember it. One way to remember it is to write a question that requires you to gather information from different sentences or paragraphs.*	Listen attentively and respond to teacher prompts and questions. Students may be asked to recall what a Right-There question is and why it should be written. They may tell a partner or answer aloud to the entire class.

2. Overview of How to Write Think-and-Search Questions

TEACHER ACTION	STUDENT ACTION
Explain how to write a Think-and-Search question. • Identify important information from different sentences or paragraphs in the passage. This will be the answer to your Think-and-Search question. • Write a question that requires the answer you identified.	Listen attentively and respond to teacher prompts and questions.

3. Model How to Write Think-and-Search Questions

Writing and answering Think-and-Search questions requires building several skills.

- Students must be able to recognize related information presented in different sections of the passage.
- Students must be able to synthesize information across these different sections (a higher-level thinking skill).
- Students must identify a question that requires multiple pieces of information to be used in the answer.

These skills alone can be difficult for struggling readers who may require additional instruction.

TEACHER ACTION	STUDENT ACTION
I am interested in something that was mentioned in a few places in the text—the lightning rod. Read a short section of text. *I am going to read the sections about lightning rods aloud* (first paragraph and section entitled "The Lightning Rod and Other Inventions"). *Follow along while I read.* Show students one to two examples of Think-and-Search questions. *We learned a lot about the lightning rod. I'm most interested in remembering why Franklin invented it. So, my question will read, "Why did Ben Franklin invent the lightning rod?"* Display the passage and use a highlighter to identify information to answer the question. *I remember that in the first paragraph, the author said that lightning strikes can cause fires and that these fires caused by lightning were a large concern for people.* *In the "Lightning Rod and Other Inventions" section, it says that other people's safety mattered to Ben.* *Now, using the information from two different sections, I can answer the question, Why did Ben Franklin invent the lightning rod?* Write the answer to the question. *I am going to write a complete sentence to answer my question.* *Ben Franklin invented the lightning rod because he cared about people's safety and the lightning rod prevented one of people's biggest fears—fires caused by lightning.*	Students either follow along while the teacher reads aloud or read the passage silently to themselves. Students provide input as directed by the teacher.

4. Practice How to Write Think-and-Search Questions

TEACHER ACTION	STUDENT ACTION
Continue modeling and engaging students in guided practice of writing Think-and-Search questions until a majority of the class can write and answer their own questions. *Now, I want you to write a Think-and-Search question on your own. Remember, you need to identify information that is provided in two or more different sentences or paragraphs and write a question about that information.* *Read the section entitled "Kite Experiment" and "The Lightning Rod and Other Inventions." I want you to consider how the kite experiment and the lightning rod are similar and write a question about it.* You may choose to provide some question stems to assist students. How are ___ and ___ similar? How are ___ and ___ different? What are the different ways that __? Exhibit 2.8 provides a sample of how students might fill in a Think-and-Search log. Monitor student work and provide feedback and guidance. As you monitor, note students who have written high-quality questions. Ask these students to share their questions with the class. Discuss why their questions are of high quality.	Students participate in guided practice activities. Students read the paragraphs and • Identify information in two or more different sentences or paragraphs • Write a question that requires them to use all of the information in the answer Students read passages and write (and answer) Think-and-Search questions. They may work independently, with a partner, or in small groups.

EXHIBIT 2.8. Think-and-Search Questions Example

Name _____ Date _____

A Think-and-Search question is one that requires you to look in two different places to find the answer. Read the following passage, then write a Think-and-Search question using information from the paragraph. Be sure to answer your question as well.

Have you ever seen what lightning can do when it strikes a building? It is so powerful that a strike can cause buildings and other structures to erupt in flames. During Ben Franklin's time, fires from lightning were a large concern for people. This is one reason he wanted to study lightning. Franklin was one of the greatest scientists of his time. Indeed, his work and experiments resulted in several important discoveries and inventions.

Ben Franklin was born in Boston, Massachusetts, on January 17, 1706. One of seventeen children, his father could afford to send him to school for only one year, so he went to work for his brother, a printer. While there, Ben read many books and taught himself to become a good writer. When he was seventeen, he ran away to Philadelphia, Pennsylvania, where he performed many of his science experiments. In addition, he helped draft, or write, the Constitution of the United States of America and, as a result, is known as one of this country's forefathers. He died in 1790 at the age of eighty-four.

Write one Think-and-Search question (and answer) using information from the paragraph.

What are two reasons Ben Franklin is famous?

He helped the country by conducting scientific experiments and he was a co-author of the Constitution of the U.S.A.

LESSON INSTRUCTIONAL GUIDE:
Question Generation—Author-and-You Questions

1. Tell Students About Author-and-You Questions

What is it?

Why use it?

TEACHER ACTION	STUDENT ACTION
Explain what Author-and-You questions are and why students should learn to write them.	Listen attentively and respond to teacher prompts and questions.
You are in the process of learning how to write three types of questions to help you remember different types of information from your reading.	Students may be asked to recall what a Right-There question is and why it should be written. They may tell a partner or answer aloud to the entire class.
The first type of question was called a Right-There question because the answer is "right there" in the text. These are usually facts.	
The second type of question was called a Think-and-Search question. These require you to identify information in two or more sentences or paragraphs that can be used to answer the question.	Students may be asked to recall what a Think-and-Search question is and why it should be written. They may tell a partner or answer aloud to the entire class.
Today, you will be learning how to write Author-and-You questions. These questions require you to use some information the author provides combined with some information you already know in order to answer. You answer these questions quite often in language arts, science, and social studies. Let me show you what an Author-and-You question looks like.	

2. Overview of How to Write Author-and-You Questions

TEACHER ACTION	STUDENT ACTION
Explain how to write an Author-and-You question. • Identify important information from the passage that makes you wonder or ponder. • Write a question that requires the answer you identified. Explain what question words are usually found at the beginning of an Author-and-You question. *Author-and-You questions often begin with the question words* why *or* how. *If you get stuck trying to think of a good Author-and-You question, try starting the question with* why *or* how.	Listen attentively and respond to teacher prompts and questions.

3. Model How to Write Author-and-You Questions

TEACHER ACTION	STUDENT ACTION
Show students one to two examples of Author-and-You questions.	Allow students to provide ideas.
Here is an example of an Author-and-You question: "What would you do to protect yourself if you were caught in a thunderstorm?"	Students may follow along or assist in writing the answer.
Identify information from the text that can be used to answer the question.	
We learned about several things that attract lightning during a thunderstorm. One of those is tall buildings. Another is a kite flying in the air. Another is a lightning rod. We also learned that metal conducts electricity.	
Identify information that students must infer in order to answer the question.	
Now, we have to use what we learned from the passage and apply it to our own lives. All of the items in the passage that attract lightning are tall. Some are metal. So, what types of things would you stay away from?	
Tall trees, metal things inside and outside the house.	
Model writing the answer to the question.	
There are several things I would do to protect myself during a thunderstorm. I would avoid standing under tall trees, and would avoid being near, sitting on, or standing on metal things.	

4. Practice How to Write Author-and-You Questions

TEACHER ACTION	STUDENT ACTION
Continue modeling and engaging students in guided practice of writing Author-and-You questions until a majority of the class can write and answer their own questions.	Students participate in guided practice activities.
Now, you will write some Author-and-You questions on your own. Remember to identify important information from the passage that makes you wonder and then write a question about it.	Students read passages and write (and answer) Author-and-You questions. They may work independently, with a partner, or in small groups.
The passage talks about items that are conductors. I wonder what other items that I use during the day may be conductors or nonconductors. See if you can write a question related to that idea.	
Exhibit 2.9 provides a sample of how students might fill in an Author-and-You log.	
Monitor student work and provide feedback and guidance. As you monitor, note students who have written high-quality questions. Ask these students to share their questions with the class. Discuss why their questions are of high quality.	

EXHIBIT 2.9. Author-and-You Questions Example

Name _____ Date _____

An Author-and-You question is one that requires you to use some information the author provides combined with some information you already know in order to answer. Read the following passage, then write an Author-and-You question using information from the paragraph. Be sure to answer your question as well.

> To make the kite Ben fastened his silk handkerchief to two strips of wood tied in a cross. Next, he attached a foot-long wire to the vertical, or upright, stick. He tied a long string to the kite and sent it into the sky. Finally, a silk ribbon went on the end of the string as a handhold to protect Ben. He also tied a metal key on the string close to the silk ribbon. According to his hypothesis, the wire would conduct the electricity from the clouds through the kite, string, and key.
>
> From his previous experiments, Ben knew that objects such as pointed metal rods could conduct electricity better than other things, such as wood or silk.

Write one Author-and-You question (and answer) using information from the paragraph.

What do you think might be some good conductors and some poor conductors?

I think a metal plate and a copper wire are good conductors. I think rubber and a dry sponge are poor conductors.

LESSON INSTRUCTIONAL GUIDE:
Review and Teacher-Led Whole-Class Wrap Up

◆ *Time:* The review step is quick—just two to three minutes. Students take about one minute to write down their review statements and another one to two minutes to share them. Teachers might also ask students to write a summary of what they read, in which case students would need more time.

The time needed for a whole-class Wrap Up varies depending on how many follow-up activities the teacher adds.

◆ *When:* After reading, after Question Generation

◆ *How:* During teacher-led modeling and guided practice, students are highly engaged in contributing to class work and practice. Once students master writing review statements, they may write independently or while working in their groups. They justify why they think their statements reflect the most important information in the text.

◆ *Purpose:* The purpose of review is to identify and remember key information from the text. The purposes of the whole-class Wrap Up are to revisit important information, help students make connections with other lessons, engage in higher-level thinking activities using the information learned, and to clarify misunderstandings.

1. Tell Students About the Review

What is it?

Why use it?

TEACHER ACTION	STUDENT ACTION
Explain what the review is and why students need to engage in review activities.	Listen attentively.

2. Overview of How to Engage in a Review and Wrap Up

TEACHER ACTION	STUDENT ACTION
Explain the steps for review: • Review the text or information on the learning log. • Write one or two sentences containing the most important information about the text. • Share review statements with the group, stating why the information is important. • Engage in a whole-class wrap up discussion.	Listen attentively.

3. Model Writing a Short Summary for Review

One way to increase the difficulty of the summary writing task is to require longer written responses. At some grade levels, being able to write strong summaries is an important objective.

TEACHER ACTION	STUDENT ACTION
Model reviewing text or learning log. *I am going to look back at my learning log to identify the most important information that I want to remember from this passage. My gist statements contain the most important information from each section, so that is a good place to start.* Model prewriting in the form of listing important information in note form. *As I read my gists, I'm going to jot down a list of information that I think is most important.* *Ben Franklin was a great scientist.* *He proved that lightning can be conducted from a storm cloud to the ground.* *He cared about people.* *He invented many things to help others (stove, glasses, lightning rod).* Model creating a two-sentence summary that contains the most important information. *For my two-sentence summary, I will include interesting information that is most important to the topic. The most important person to remember is Ben Franklin, so he will be the subject of my first sentence.* *"Franklin used his knowledge about positive and negative electrical charges and the different conduction properties of objects to prove that lightning is electricity."* *Now, I want to remember what he invented as a result of his discovery.* *"With his knowledge and experiments, he invented the lightning rod to protect people by increasing the safety of their homes, churches, and ships."*	Listen attentively and follow teacher's prompts.

4. Practice Writing a Short Summary for Review

TEACHER ACTION	STUDENT ACTION
Look back at several previously read passages. Practice reviewing key information in the text, prewriting, and writing a two-sentence summary.	Listen attentively and follow teacher's prompts.

5. Teacher-Led Wrap Up

TEACHER ACTION	STUDENT ACTION
Lead a discussion that requires students to use the information they learned in the passage to draw conclusions, form opinions, or take a different perspective. Also, use this time to clarify any misunderstanding and reinforce key ideas. Some possible discussion questions for the sample passage are as follows: Draw conclusions: *Why did Ben Franklin become interested in proving that lightning was indeed electricity?* Form opinions: *What was Ben Franklin's most important invention and why?* Take a different perspective: *Imagine you were Ben Franklin during the kite experiment. Explain how you felt before the experiment. During the experiment. When you made the discovery.*	Follow teacher's prompts and engage in a discussion. Students write down what they learned with teacher guidance, independently, with a partner, or in small groups.

As you teach the CSR strategies through modeling, guided practice, and independent practice, you will find that some students learn to use the strategies rather easily. Others may struggle for some time. We encourage you to continue challenging your entire class with new strategy-learning and practice opportunities using engaging text while at the same time attending to individual student needs. In subsequent chapters, you will learn to do both by engaging students in cooperative learning and using student data to inform instructional decisions. Finally, these lessons are meant to give you an idea of how to teach CSR strategies. There is room for creativity in how you present each strategy. We encourage you to enliven your classroom with exciting lesson delivery and compelling reading materials that bring CSR to life.

CHAPTER 3

Implementing CSR Cooperative Learning

> *[CSR] has been an incredible innovation in my teaching. . . . I hadn't done cooperative groups in middle school language arts before, and it's incredible.*
>
> —**MIDDLE SCHOOL LANGUAGE ARTS TEACHER**

> *When you are instructing the large group, seated like they are right now [separately], you have those that are sitting here doodling or writing a note to their friend or whatever but when they are in the CSR group, they have to focus because they each have a job and without that job, nothing gets done. . . . So I think the focus is better [with CSR] and when their focus is better, then you don't have the behavior issues because they don't have time to do that.*
>
> —**MIDDLE SCHOOL LANGUAGE ARTS TEACHER**

Ms. Jones has twenty-seven students in her class. According to the school district's designations, ten students are ELLs (native languages: six Spanish, two Chinese, one Russian, and one Nepalese), two have learning disabilities, one student has ADHD, and two are gifted and talented. Within this diverse classroom, a range of reading skills is represented. Throughout the week, Ms. Jones provides many opportunities for her students to collaborate on assignments, to share ideas with one another, and to discuss what they are learning. During CSR, Ms. Jones uses cooperative learning. In her classroom, you might notice that when students are working in small groups, only one voice in a group is heard at a time. In their CSR groups, students work together, leaning forward to listen to one another, discussing their reading and CSR strategies. When students are thinking on their own and writing in their learning logs, it is very quiet. Ms. Jones brings students together during Preview and Review and sometimes between sections to share a clunk or to evaluate student gists. She calls on students to respond (rather than asking for volunteers) or asks for a choral response or uses other response options that engage many students at once. Ms. Jones and her students are familiar with

---

EXHIBIT 3.1. Cooperative Learning Resources

Aronson, E., & Patnoe, S. (1997). *The jigsaw classroom: Building cooperation in the classroom* (2nd ed.). New York: Addison Wesley Longman.

Johnson, D., & Johnson, R. (2000). *Learning together and alone* (5th ed.). Edina, MN: Interaction Book Company.

Kagan, S., & Kagan, M. (2009). *Kagan cooperative learning.* San Clemente, CA: Kagan Publishing.

Klingner, J., Vaughn, S., Dimino, J., Schumm, J., & Bryant, D. (2001). *Collaborative strategic reading: Strategies for improving comprehension* (ch. 3). Longmont, CO: Sopris West.

Marzano, R., Pickering, D., & Pollock, J. (2001). *Classroom instruction that works: Research-based strategies for increasing student achievement.* Alexandria, VA: Association for Supervision and Curriculum Development.

Sharan, S. (ed.). (1994). *Handbook of cooperative learning methods.* Westport, CT: Greenwood Press.

Slavin, R. (1983). *Cooperative learning.* New York: Longman.

---

the CSR routines that structure discussions and activities. Although topics and content vary according to the curriculum, in each CSR lesson students are busy, active, and engaged, and so is Ms. Jones.

Cooperative learning provides a structure for the student small-group activities that are woven through many effective interventions, including CSR. In this chapter, we focus on the steps needed to establish and maintain effective cooperative learning during CSR instruction. We do not cover cooperative learning in depth but rather focus on how to set up and use cooperative learning in a CSR classroom. For additional information about cooperative learning and the research that supports this model of instruction, see Exhibit 3.1.

Step One: Set Up for Success

The purpose of step one is for teachers to understand the goals of cooperative learning with CSR and how the associated CSR materials and supports provide a structure for effective group work. In addition, teachers learn to distinguish between other forms of group work and the cooperative group work that occurs in CSR lessons.

CSR and its accompanying materials were developed to support four foundational features of cooperative learning:[1] positive interdependence, promoting interaction, individual accountability, and social skills. Table 3.1 provides a brief explanation of each

TABLE 3.1. CSR Cooperative Learning: Features and Supports

FEATURES OF COOPERATIVE LEARNING	CSR SUPPORTS
Positive interdependence: Each student is a valued and contributing member of the group. Without *each* group member, the CSR group could not function effectively.	• CSR group roles • Norms for group work
Promoting interaction: CSR strategy implementation, timing, and teacher feedback are designed to promote peer interaction within cooperative groups.	• CSR strategies • CSR learning logs • Norms for group work • Teacher feedback
Individual accountability: Successful cooperative learning holds all students responsible for actively participating in discussions and for producing their own work.	• CSR learning logs • Student resource materials • Lesson timing to ensure think, write, and wait time
Cooperative social skills: Students must know how to interact within a CSR group. Expectations are clear and explicit instruction is provided in areas such as sharing, listening attentively, asking clarifying questions, and giving feedback.	• Student roles • Norms for group work

TABLE 3.2. What CSR Cooperative Learning Is and Is Not

WHAT IT IS	WHAT IT IS NOT
• Students are strategically placed in heterogeneous, mixed-ability groups. • Each member has an assigned role. • Group task is very specific. • Each individual is responsible for own learning and group learning. • Students partake in higher-order thinking skills beyond which they could have accomplished by themselves. • Teacher promotes peer interactions through explicit teaching and feedback.	• Students are placed randomly in groups. • Students work on their own assignments while sitting at the same table. • Group roles and tasks are undefined. • There is little individual or group accountability. • Each student does less work than they would have done on their own. • Students are on their own during group-work time with little support from the teacher.

feature and the associated supportive CSR structures. Although each method of cooperative learning puts its own spin on these features, all use core principles to promote active engagement and equal participation by every member of the group.

During professional development (PD), we suggest providing teachers with this table of cooperative learning features and supports as well as Table 3.2, "What CSR Cooperative Learning Is and Is Not." Teachers benefit from reviewing this information and having the opportunity to discuss what group work currently looks like in their classes and how CSR cooperative learning is similar to and different from what they do already. You will learn more about CSR professional development in Chapter Five. Additional questions for participants might include the following:

- What aspects of student group work in your class support CSR cooperative learning features?
- What aspects of student group work are not working as well?

Many teachers display Table 3.2 as a poster and refer to it with students as they establish norms for group work during CSR. As teachers get ready to use CSR in their classrooms, they prepare the following materials and supports: CSR cue cards, CSR learning logs, and CSR forms (available in Appendix A).

Step Two: Assign Students to Groups

Assigning students to heterogeneous groups and arranging the room to support group work is an important step. There are many formulas for creating effective student groups for cooperative learning. First, group size matters. The standard cooperative group consists of four students, each with one CSR role: Leader, Clunk Expert, Gist Expert, and Question Expert. Although teachers may play around with group size, four seems to be a target number in which students can actively engage in rich discussion when sitting at desks or in chairs that can be arranged to promote participation. As additional group members are added, the participation opportunities go down. Not only does it take longer to share and discuss as groups get larger, but it also makes it easier for one or more of the students to sit back and do less while the other group members carry the discussion. In most cases, when class numbers do not add up to even groups of four, having several groups of four with a few groups of three is preferable to groups that are larger than four. For example, a class of thirty-one students can be divided into seven groups of four students and one group of three. A student can perform more than one role if necessary (e.g., Clunk Expert and Question Expert).

Much attention has been given to the question of how to assign students to groups. Regardless of which system you use, the key to remember is that groups should represent a balance of students in terms of academic skills, gender, social skills, language proficiency, cultural background, and consideration of individual student traits (e.g., personalities, friendships, energy level) that influence how well a group of students will be able to work together. The following steps provide one way of assigning students to groups.[2]

1. First, rank-order students by reading ability or academic achievement level. Teachers may use state assessment reading scores, information from class-administered tests or assignments, or their knowledge of students' reading levels. The purpose of this process is to create groups that represent a range of achievement levels. See Form 3.1.

2. Identify your leaders. Put a star next to the name of students who have the motivation and skills to be a group leader. Note that leaders aren't necessarily the highest achievers in your class. Leaders often possess strong communication skills, they are respectful to and respected by others, follow directions, and are

FORM 3.1. Assigning Students to CSR Groups

STUDENT NAME (RANK ORDERED)	LEADERS	NOTES
1.		
2.		
3.		
4.		
5.		
6.		
7.		
8.		
9.		
10.		
11.		
12.		
13.		
14.		
15.		
16.		
17.		
18.		
19.		
20.		
21.		
22.		
23.		
24.		
25.		
26.		
27.		
28.		
29.		
30.		
31.		
32.		
33.		
34.		
35.		

EXHIBIT 3.2. Using Note Cards to Create Student Groups

Class Rank _____

Student Name _____

Leader _____ Notes _____

_____

self-regulated learners. Leaders may or may not be strong readers. Each CSR group will have one student who has been identified as a leader. As students become more familiar with CSR and the CSR roles, other students (who may not be "natural" leaders) will be able to assume the role of the leader during CSR.

3. Identify any specific student information that could influence group configurations:

    a. Language level

    b. Friends or enemies

    c. Special learning needs

    d. Bossy, easily off-task, quiet, overly independent, and so on

4. Select the groups. Select two students from the top half of the list and two students from the bottom half of the list, checking to be sure you have one starred leader and a group of students who you believe will work well together. Create the rest of the groups. As you finalize your groups, be sure to confirm that students are of different genders, reflect the ethnic and cultural diversity of your class, and that you have taken into account the student information notes in your selection process. Adjust as needed. Some teachers prefer to put student information on note cards so they can physically manipulate the groupings. Exhibit 3.2 shows how note cards can be used.

How Long Should Students Remain in the Same Group?

We recommend that students stay in the same groups for about six to nine weeks, though teachers have reported changing groups more frequently (every three weeks) and others maintain that groups can stay the same for an entire school year. There are many components that influence how quickly students can gel in a group such as how well students know each other, how similar they are to one another in their learning and communication styles, and the classroom climate that has been established prior to introducing CSR cooperative group work. The goal is for students to take the time to develop cohesion and trust. In time, students experience authentic conversations about text and feel comfortable contributing and giving feedback to their fellow group members.

How Often Should Students Switch Roles?

When teachers are getting CSR up and running, it is helpful to assign roles and for students to perform their same role for several CSR lessons. With the exception of the Leader role, which requires just a bit more attention and focus, once students are proficient at CSR, they seem to be able to move easily between the various roles, even assuming more than one role if they are in a small group or if a group member is absent. Recall that in CSR, all students actively participate in each component, so after a while students are not fussy about which role they have because they all share the work and the responsibility for learning.

How Do I Group English Language Learners?

A common challenge that teachers ask about is how to group ELLs in CSR. ELLs benefit in a variety of ways in CSR groups. They have frequent opportunities to practice and develop their English language skills, they hear models of English from students who are proficient in English, and they receive in-the-moment support from other students in their group. We suggest focusing on using heterogeneous groups so that all students in the class are provided with structured opportunities to interact with and learn from a variety of their peers. If possible, ELLs also benefit from having another student in their group who is bilingual in the same language(s) so that native language can be used to facilitate understanding.

What About Students Who Are Gifted and Talented?

Students who are advanced academically benefit from cooperative learning and can be successfully integrated into CSR groups. There may be other times to differentiate instruction and to provide accelerated learning opportunities for students who are above grade level, but during CSR these students (1) benefit academically from supporting other students and facilitating understanding in the group, (2) apply higher-order thinking skills that allow them to challenge assumptions and to bring their wealth of knowledge into the discussion, and (3) develop their social skills such as taking turns, active listening, considering the viewpoints of others, and providing constructive feedback. Students who are gifted and talented will generally understand the content being taught, regardless of the presentation format. CSR cooperative groups allow these students the opportunity to think deeply about content and to engage in discussions in a socially engaging environment. Unlike with small-group work, where one student might feel as though she or he is "doing all the work," in CSR all students write in individual learning logs and are responsible for completing their own work.

How Should I Assign Struggling Readers to Cooperative Groups?

One of the benefits of CSR cooperative groups is that struggling readers are provided access to content they might not be able to read and understand on their own. Although there may be times to group students by ability (e.g., to focus on specific decoding skills), CSR affords struggling readers the opportunity to think about and discuss challenging content. Gains for struggling readers using cooperative learning and CSR have been well documented. Several aspects of cooperative learning that are important to all learners may be critical to the successful outcomes of struggling readers and students with disabilities.[3] First, struggling readers benefit from being placed in groups with peers who are helpful and supportive so they feel accepted and safe. Second, using roles also provides structure and increases engagement and participation because students know how to participate in their group and can provide valuable contributions. Struggling readers can be successful Leaders or Clunk, Gist, or Question Experts. Third, these students excel when they are explicitly taught the CSR strategies and the group-work skills needed to participate and contribute. Finally, teachers must monitor progress and provide feedback so they can identify modifications or additional instruction that may be required. As Tanya Thompson, a seventh-grade language arts teacher, noted, "CSR has been good because it gave students with special needs a way to participate. You're stopping and talking about the gist and so they're hearing it and they're reading it together. It's made a lot of levels of text very accessible for them."

How Do I Arrange the Room for Successful Group Work?

How desks or chairs are arranged is also an important element in grouping. While observing a middle school science classroom with large science lab tables, we noticed that students were only talking to the person seated next to them instead of including all four group members in discussions. We realized that even though we could join two tables together to form a group of four, the students sitting across from one another were very far away from each other. As a natural response, students informally created two groups of two students. To address this challenge, the teacher moved the two tables apart and had students move their chairs around just one table. Immediately, the group dynamic shifted, and students were able to participate in groups of four. Students need to face each other. A little work up front showing students what a cooperative group does and does not look like can go a long way. Once teachers have their classes and groups arranged, they can create a class diagram of where tables, chairs, or desks go during group work and where they go during independent work. If desks are to be moved back and forth, display the diagram for students or put tape on the floor. This will save time arranging and rearranging. Groups should also be spaced so that the teacher can make his or her way around the room to monitor students and so that students can easily get to materials they might need.

Step Three: Use CSR Roles

Roles specify and break down a task. In CSR, roles are used to structure the use of the CSR strategies and the flow of the lesson. They also provide each student with a unique responsibility that increases accountability to the group. For students, roles are like jobs and it takes many jobs to complete a project. Teachers often talk briefly with students about how various jobs work together outside of the classroom. For example, in a school there are teachers, the principal, secretaries, custodians, and so on. Without all of these individuals doing their own jobs, the school would not be able to run. If all adults in a school were teachers, who would answer the phone, help a student who scraped her knee, coordinate school assemblies and meetings, or make sure the floors were clean and tidy? Roles in CSR are integral to the success of student group work.

CSR roles have changed somewhat over time.[4] We now primarily use four basic roles: the Leader, Clunk Expert, Gist Expert, and Question Expert. Students might also serve in the role of Encourager (to provide positive feedback to the group and guide a reflection on the group process at the end) or Timekeeper. Here we describe the essential CSR roles. CSR cue cards are given to students to guide them through the responsibilities of their role. Each cue card includes a job description, a guided script of what to say and do during the selected strategy, and on the back, the card provides additional strategy resources. The cue cards are the most useful when students are learning CSR and beginning to work in their groups. As students become proficient at implementing the CSR model, they may refer occasionally to their cue card, but in general, students come to rely less on the cue card over time as they internalize the CSR process. Full-size reproducible cue cards are included in Appendix A. Exhibits 3.3 through 3.7 describe the recursive nature of each strategy and can be used to introduce teachers or students to the CSR roles as used in groups. Each strategy is guided by the use of the cue cards. It includes time for students first to think and write on their own, followed by structured sharing and discussion. Because the teacher is the leader for Preview, there is a teacher cue card instead of a student cue card for that component. Like student cue cards, teacher cue cards guide teachers through the various CSR

EXHIBIT 3.3. Preview in Groups

Begin class with students in groups.

- State the topic.
- Present important proper nouns and key vocabulary concepts (two to three).
- Students preview the text (read headings, subheadings, bold words, charts, etc.).
- Direct students to brainstorm what they know about the topic on their own.

EXHIBIT 3.4. Clunks in Groups

- Leader says, "Write down your clunks."

- Each student identifies clunks on his or her own and writes in a learning log.

- Clunk Expert guides the group to use fix-up strategies.
  - Clunk Expert says, "Who has a clunk?"
  - Clunk Expert says, "Does anyone know what the clunk means?"
  - Clunk Expert guides the group to use fix-up strategies to figure out the meaning of the clunks.

EXHIBIT 3.5. Gist in Groups

- After clunks, Leader says, "It's time to Get the Gist. Gist Expert, help us out."

- Gist Expert guides the group to Get the Gist.

- Gist Expert says, "What is the most important who or what in this section?"

- Group decides.

- Gist Expert says, "Everyone, think of your own gist and write it in your learning log."

- When students are done, Gist Expert says, "Who would like to share their gist?"

EXHIBIT 3.6. Wrap Up in Groups

- After all sections are finished
  - Leader says, "It's time to ask questions. Question Expert, help us out."
  - Question Expert says, "Let's think of some questions to check whether we really understood what we read . . ."
  - Each student writes his or her own questions and answers first.
  - Question Expert guides the students to share their questions and ask other students to answer them.

EXHIBIT 3.7. Review in Groups

- The Leader says, "It's time to review what we read. Write the one or two most important ideas that you read about today."

- Each student writes his or her own review statements.

- Leader guides students to share.

---

strategies. They provide the steps of the strategy as well as tips for monitoring student work and providing feedback (see Appendix A).

Introducing CSR Roles

Introducing roles and maintaining their use follows a similar format to how you teach other strategies and routines in your class. Students benefit from explicit instruction about what the role is, why it is important, and how to perform the role. Models of what CSR looks like when students are using roles allow students to get a glimpse of the potential of CSR groups. Finally, students need many opportunities to practice using their roles in CSR groups with informative feedback about what is working and what needs to be improved. There are many ways to introduce the CSR roles. Many teachers prefer to teach all the strategies first and then to introduce student roles. Other teachers would rather teach students the roles as they learn the strategies. Here we provide suggestions for teaching the CSR roles to students.[5]

Meet with Role-Alike Groups

Some teachers prefer to discuss roles first with students in role-alike groups. In role-alike groups, the teacher meets briefly with small groups of students who will all engage in the same role. Students review the cue card for that role, ask questions, and talk about the important aspects of their role. For each role, students address these questions:

- What are the responsibilities of someone in this role?

- Why is this role important in CSR?

After students understand their roles, they go back to their CSR groups to share and discuss their roles with their groupmates, using Form 3.2, "Our CSR Roles." They report their responses to these questions and then the group works together to answer the following question for each role:

- How do you think this role works with the other roles in CSR?

The role-alike group uses a jigsaw learning format in which each student comes back to their CSR group with unique information that they teach to their peers.[6] It sets up the notion that all members have something important to contribute to their groups. Once all students learn their roles, they are ready to begin applying them in small groups.

FORM 3.2. Our CSR Roles

1. What are the responsibilities of someone in this role?

2. Why is this role important in CSR?

3. How does this role work together with the other CSR roles?

Leader _____

_____

_____

_____

_____

_____

_____

Clunk Expert _____

_____

_____

_____

_____

_____

_____

Gist Expert _____

_____

_____

_____

_____

_____

_____

Question Expert _____

_____

_____

_____

_____

_____

_____

Build Roles with Strategies

Other teachers introduce the roles one at a time, along with the strategy. For instance, after introducing the fix-up strategies and practicing them with the entire class, the teacher then assigns a Clunk Expert to each student group. The group looks at the Clunk Expert role together, using the questions discussed previously. Then, the group practices just the Click and Clunk strategy, guided by the Clunk Expert. This is a great way to provide practice with the strategy and to introduce the role simultaneously. The value of this option is that students connect the role with the strategy. The Clunk Expert is seen as integral to the Click and Clunk strategy and thus the strategy cannot be performed without the guidance of the person in that role. Teachers can introduce each role along with the strategy, and then when all strategies have been taught, the Leader role is introduced. With all strategies and strategy roles in place, the Leader can facilitate the integration of all expert job roles with the CSR strategies to complete an entire CSR lesson.

Provide Models of CSR Group Work

Students benefit from seeing models of students working collaboratively in groups and so do teachers! In one middle school, a group of students who had learned CSR the year before practiced CSR with the teacher's guidance and then modeled group work in a class of sixth-graders who were just learning CSR. The students observing the model were given a guided "noticing" sheet so they could record student and teacher actions during CSR. The model students usually do just part of a CSR lesson, about ten minutes or so, and then they become a panel as the class debriefs about what they saw. Without the luxury of experienced student participants, other teachers have supported one group in the class to gain proficiency and then had the spotlight group model in front of the class. Other schools have videorecorded student groups and can then select video clips to show to students who are learning CSR. In one school, the teachers even videotaped themselves using roles in small groups during a CSR lesson and showed that to the students, using a similar guided noticing activity. Video clips are also useful because they can be viewed more than once for different purposes. Examples of guided noticing prompts include the following:

- Record everything you can about how students are helping each other to use the Click and Clunk strategy.
- Write down everything you can about how students use their role cards.
- Look at the CSR rules. Write down the ways in which the group in the video are following the CSR rules.
- What words are students using to give feedback to one another during this gist discussion?

Practice Roles with the Whole Class

To reinforce CSR roles, practice with the entire class as if the class were one big cooperative learning group. This demonstrates the flow and use of CSR roles, yet still allows the teacher to control the timing and the transitions from one strategy to the next. In this activity, the teacher assigns a role to four students in the class. The class then reads a text using CSR, with the four students leading the whole-class CSR group instead of the teacher. During this scaffolded grouping, the teacher can provide feedback to the class about how roles support high-quality strategy application while students "run" the lesson. The whole-class CSR practice group activity involves all students in the lesson, keeping them engaged and learning as they watch the roles being used.

Step Four: Teach Routines and Group-Work Skills

In the opening class example, the students appeared to run the show. They were engaged and on task every minute of the class period. At the end of a CSR lesson, students have worked hard and they have learned quite a bit about the text and the topic they have pursued that day. If all went well, they probably had fun as they worked together and discussed with their peers. But this well-oiled machine has a powerful engineer behind it—the teacher. And although students gain independence as they become proficient at applying CSR strategies and working together in cooperative groups, the teacher continues to encourage effective peer interaction, to promote high-quality CSR strategy use, and to facilitate content learning.

Lucas:	All right, I have shrill and disembarked.
Amy:	Same here.
Gabriel (Clunk Expert):	Me, too.
Amy:	All right.
Heidi:	I had shrill.
Gabriel:	All right, shrill . . . Let's reread the sentence *(reads from text)*.
Amy:	I think that's like . . . I don't know.
Heidi:	Well, insects make different noises, so maybe it's an insect noise.
Amy:	I thought it was like a scream.
Heidi:	Or like something that sounds bad in your ears . . .

Gabriel:	Yeah . . . I don't know . . .
Heidi:	So, maybe a . . . bad sound? Or a screechy sound maybe?
Gabriel:	That works.
Lucas:	What strategy was that?
Heidi:	Ah, number one, because we reread the sentence. And also background knowledge.
Teacher (stopping by and listening in):	Excellent job working together to figure out your clunk. Yes, you thought about what was in the text and also your background knowledge.

Routines

Routines help make group work manageable for the teacher and the students. The amount of time needed to teach routines varies by class and many teachers easily integrate routines that are already in place in their class. The following routines are taught to structure group work:

- Get into groups quickly with all necessary materials.
- Store and manage CSR materials (e.g., student folders, table materials, tab in student's binder).
- Manage the flow of the lesson (e.g., timer).
- Gain students' attention when they are in groups.
- Follow CSR rules:
  - Talk only about CSR.
  - Talk only to members of your group.
  - Use only library voices.
  - If someone has a question, the Leader raises his or her hand.

Routines are all about practice and reinforcement and the one responsible for making sure they stick is the teacher. Too often, students are blamed for off-task behavior when there may be more the teacher can do to create consistent and predictable routines. Consider how a teacher might use a timer to control the flow of a CSR lesson. We observed one teacher who was initially good at setting the timer and explaining to students the procedure for first checking in and then moving on to the next strategy. But, when the timer went off, time and again, the teacher would ignore it, wrapped up with one student or a small group and taking her attention away from the rest of the groups who were quickly becoming unfocused and moving into off-topic conversations. It was then difficult for the teacher to rein the students back in. In a coaching session, the coach shared with the teacher her observations of how much time was lost with the off-task behavior (six minutes past the four-minute timer allotment) and the additional efforts to regain order in the class (three minutes to quiet the rumble). With practice, the teacher became comfortable with the timer and used it more systematically. The students knew what to expect and began to work more efficiently within the amount of time they were given. Transitions were smooth because students were coming back together from a discussion of the text and knew what was coming next.

Group-Work Skills

Group-work skills are at the core of cooperative learning. Students need to know how to work together and to do so efficiently. The application of group-work skills allows students to apply critical-thinking skills to build understanding. Many teachers provide instruction in the following group-work skills:

- Develop a safe environment for group work (e.g., build trust, community).
- Resolve conflicts that arise in the group.
- Foster think and write time.
- Take turns sharing in the group.
- Share your ideas with your group members.
- Engage in high-quality discussions (e.g., provide positive feedback, ask for clarification, disagree politely, build on others' responses).

Teachers may choose to use a minilesson format to introduce and to practice essential group-work skills. The lesson planning guide shown in Exhibit 3.8 can help teachers identify skills that need to be taught with a plan for how to introduce, practice, and maintain the skills. Often, the introduction of a skill can be quite short, taking only about five to ten minutes. In Exhibit 3.8, a teacher decided to conduct a minilesson that focuses on sharing in CSR groups.

The development of group-work skills varies and instruction should be customized to meet student needs. For example, Mrs. Harmon, a middle school teacher, shared that her seventh-grade students were working well together and engaging in productive CSR discussions. These students were, as she put it, "running with CSR." They "can't wait to get into their groups." At the same time, she noted that her sixth-graders hadn't yet solidified who they would become in middle school. They were unsure of themselves and less comfortable taking risks and opening up with one another. Mrs. Harmon chose to initiate several team-building minilessons that focused on providing opportunities for students to get to know each other and to establish a common ground. After a few of these brief activities, students were ready to get into CSR groups and to begin the work of unpacking academic content together.

EXHIBIT 3.8. Minilesson: Sharing During Group Work

FOCUS SKILL: Sharing during group work	
1. Define and model the skill.	Sharing in a group
2. Help students see the relevance of the skill.	Sharing is a basic group skill that is necessary for groups to function effectively. If students can't share, they will not be able to discuss the text or the quality of their strategy use. Sharing sets the expectation that during group work all students take turns, participate, listen, and learn from each other. Ask students to provide examples of sharing, such as brainstorming ideas or sharing a favorite part of a book or a favorite movie.
3. Have students describe the skill.	Have student make a list of words that describe sharing in groups: take turns, only one person talks at a time, participate, list information, listen, learn, don't comment, and so on. Have two students volunteer to share their list in front of the class. Have students face each other. Provide one minute for students to take turns sharing their lists.
4. Discuss and reinforce students' efforts.	Debrief with the class. Here the teacher and students can point out the benefits of sharing and also the limitations. For example, during sharing, you just listen, you do not provide feedback or build on others' ideas. Talk with the class about the difference between sharing and discussion and when each might be used in CSR. In CSR, sharing usually happens during brainstorming and predicting, whereas discussion occurs during Click and Clunk, Get the Gist, and Wrap Up.
5. Have students practice the skill.	Have students practice sharing during the Preview and highlight the important skills they are applying.
6. Maintain use of skill with follow-up practice.	Continue to reinforce sharing and to contrast when students are sharing instead of discussing. If students only share their gists, they will not have the opportunity to evaluate their quality or to work together to improve their work.

Step Five: Facilitate Group Work

As students begin to use CSR roles and to work in their small groups, there are many ways that teachers can support rich discussions and increase the quality of student-led group work. Facilitating group work begins with the roles, routines, and group-work skills that are described in previous sections, but teachers provide ongoing support that promotes peer interaction and discussion. It may seem counterintuitive that one area that supports group work is the teacher-led Preview, the start of the lesson when the teacher is in front of the class. The teacher-led Preview is so important because it is here that the teacher introduces the lesson, builds background knowledge, helps students make connections to their own understanding, and focuses students on the important components of the text. A strong Preview sparks students' interest in the text and sets the tone for the lesson. During Preview, students also begin the group-work process when they share their brainstorm and prediction ideas with one another. Once students are in their groups, the teacher shapes the depth of discussion through the feedback that is provided to students. The following sections describe several tips about how to provide important feedback to students.

Be Specific

Mr. Lance wanted to help his students during CSR group work but did not know how. A strong teacher and great leader in the class, he revealed that he was lost during group work, not knowing how to foster discussion or to assist students. He often approached a group with a vague question such as, "How's it going?" to which the students would commonly respond, "Fine." Then Mr. Lance was stuck. If the kids were fine, and he just asked if they were, what could he do to support them in their work? After a few suggestions, Mr. Lance was able to offer feedback to students while still valuing that they were leading the group. Mr. Lance learned to approach a group without saying anything at first. He would stand or sit with them for thirty seconds or so and just listen. Once he had a sense for where the students were in CSR and in their discussion, he could ask a focused question or provide specific feedback. Comments overheard in his room were as follows:

- How did you use fix-up strategies to come up with your definition for the word *chronology*?
- In what way is Henry's gist different from yours?
- That's a great question because it makes a connection between what we are reading today about Darth Vader being an antihero and what we have been learning about how heroes are portrayed in literature.

Use the CSR Strategies to Guide Feedback

Evident in the examples from Mr. Lance's class are the connections he makes to CSR strategies. With this feedback he is also able to promote peer interaction. Rather than coming into a group and "teaching" students, the teacher coaches students to engage in discussion, using their CSR roles. For instance, when a student struggled with the word *disembark*, Mr. Lance asked, "Clunk Expert, what does your group need to do first?" In this way, the teacher empowers the students to use their reading strategies and each other instead of relying on the teacher to provide the correct answer. An important goal of CSR is to increase students' comprehension by developing their strategy toolkit. Students apply strategies to repair their own misunderstandings and to synthesize and remember what they read. The role of the teacher during group work is to facilitate the use of these tools by students and to support students to think and discuss what they are reading.

Model Appropriate Group-Work Skills

Research has demonstrated that student discourse follows the model that teachers provide.[7] Thus, teachers should pay attention to what they are saying and how they are participating in groups. Behaviors such as using a quiet voice (following CSR rules), waiting for a pause before speaking (taking turns), nodding one's head or saying, "umm hmmm" when a student is talking (active listening), and asking for clarification such as, "Why do you think that is the most important idea?" (using discussion skills) provide examples of appropriate group-work behaviors that students can replicate. Though at times the teacher may guide students to make connections or to come to an understanding, there is thought to modeling the skills teachers would like students to use rather than employing other common teacher behaviors, such as dominating the discussion, nominating who will speak, or interrupting.

Promote Peer Interaction

A useful distinction for teachers and students is understanding the difference between sharing and discussion. Sharing is a basic group-work skill, without which groups could not function. Though listening is involved, sharing essentially involves students offering their ideas, as occurs during brainstorming. Typically, students do not need to debate or question connections to prior knowledge. However, not every gist captures the main idea of a section. Students often need to decide together the most important information and then debate the quality of individual gists in their groups. Discussion is a higher-level skill that includes the give and take of ideas, providing feedback, and clarifying responses, and students may be more likely to discuss when they are encouraged to do so by the teacher.

In addition to teaching students the skills they need to discuss with one another, teachers can promote peer interaction through the feedback they provide. Sometimes students just skip the discussion. Other times, when students disagree they may turn to the teacher for help. In the following example, the teacher cues the Gist Expert, who in turn leads the group to decide on their own the most important ideas in the section in preparation for writing their gists.

Jaime (Gist Expert):	OK, so, let's go to the gist. Does anybody have any important ideas about this section?
Lucy:	Well, this is actually talking more about the North Pole, although it mentioned the South Pole. It was talking about the north and it was telling about the effects that it did.
Sara:	Yeah and 65 percent loss of the ice and two different ice types; it was talking about that, too.
Jaime:	Where's that?
Sara:	See, the sea ice is melting *(reading).*
Tonio:	It was talking about how it shattered all previous records of this significant arctic ice.
Jaime:	'Cause it—
Lucy:	Caused the loss of 65 percent of the ice. That's like really important and especially if it happened just that one year.
Jaime:	That's more than half. Are we ready to write now?

Students are social by nature. They enjoy sharing, discussing, and interacting with peers. But not all students know how to use these social skills in academic settings. Talking about challenging content, working together with a common goal, and being responsible for carrying out the work without a teacher leading every step of the way is new territory for many students. Features of cooperative learning are built into CSR so teachers have the materials and structures in place to support cooperative learning. With explicit instruction, monitoring, and feedback, cooperative learning with CSR is a productive, engaging, and motivating way to learn.

CHAPTER 4

Using Student Data to Inform Instructional Decisions

> *And the learning logs. Oh, my gosh! The learning logs helped me so much. I knew what I needed to look for in order to give them a grade, and how to grade those, because I wasn't really sure with reciprocal reading, you know, because with reciprocal reading they would only write down whatever their job was and then with the next chapter they would switch jobs and write that down. But with the learning logs in CSR everybody had to write down everything, so I was really able to see their progress in all of their groups.*
>
> **—Middle school language arts teacher**

> *Out of all the stuff we do in this class, I like CSR the most because I like reading and working with partners.*
>
> **—Seventh-grade student**

Effective teachers realize that the most important test of whether they have taught a successful lesson is if their students learned what they set out to teach. They question whether their students were engaged, if they ignited their thinking, and if they met lesson objectives. During and after a CSR lesson, teachers ask themselves the following questions:

- How do I know whether my students understand what I have taught?
- How do I identify the struggling students and then decide what to reteach them?
- How do I answer my principal's questions about whether or not CSR is working in my classroom?

In this chapter, we describe how to use student data to inform instructional decisions. We focus on two ways in particular: progress monitoring and learning logs. When teachers understand what each of their students know and can do, they are able to accelerate learning for students who excel and provide reteaching and extended learning opportunities for students who struggle. When teachers are well supplied with student data, they are in a better position to communicate with their principals and others about the success of CSR in their classrooms. They also have concrete information to share with parents about their students' successes and needs.

Progress-Monitoring Checks

Monitoring students' progress while they are learning to use reading comprehension strategies is an important part of successful implementation of CSR. We have developed a series of progress-monitoring checks and a simple procedure that can be implemented in elementary, middle, and high school to guide instruction. We describe one teacher's experiences collecting and analyzing progress monitoring data followed by a section on how to remediate difficulties that students experience using small-group instruction and effective feedback. We also offer a set of resources to use when implementing progress monitoring and instructional decision-making plans.

First, consider Mrs. Clark's experience. She is a seventh-grade social studies teacher who is teaching her students CSR strategies so they may better comprehend content area material. Her goal is for students to engage in all CSR strategies within the cooperative group setting as well as use the strategies during independent work time and test taking.

Mrs. Clark recently taught her students to write Right-There questions. You may recall that Right-There questions are ones in which students can find the answer explicitly in the text. She has modeled the strategy for generating these question types and has provided guided and independent practice. Now, she wonders whether or not her class is ready to learn a new question type, who in her class has an adequate grasp of the strategy, and who needs additional instruction.

At the end of class, she administers a progress-monitoring check, giving students approximately five minutes to work (see filled-in example in Exhibit 2.7).

After class, Mrs. Clark reviews the progress-monitoring checks and makes four stacks of papers: (1) students who write high-quality Right-There questions, (2) students who write adequate Right-There questions, (3) students who need guided practice with Right-There questions, and (4) students who need considerable instruction and practice writing Right-There questions. Here is what Mrs. Clark learned about her students' understanding of Right-There questions:

GROUP	NUMBER OF STUDENTS
Students who can write high-quality Right-There questions	5
Students who can write adequate Right-There questions	12
Students who need guided practice writing Right-There questions	3
Students who need considerable instruction and practice writing Right-There questions	3

Based on this information, Mrs. Clark planned her instruction for the next day. She decided to set aside twenty minutes at the beginning of class to implement the following instruction:

GROUP	NUMBER OF STUDENTS	INSTRUCTIONAL PLAN
Students who can write adequate and high-quality Right-There questions	17	• Can practice CSR group work • Are provided a slightly more difficult passage • Work in small groups to complete the CSR strategies • Work together to develop improved Right-There questions
Students who need guided practice writing Right-There questions	3	• Work with the teacher in a small group • Provide several short passages • Watch teacher model writing Right-There questions • Spend most of the time writing Right-There questions with guided practice
Students who struggle writing Right-There questions	3	

Similar procedures for progress monitoring can be applied to each of the elements of CSR. Students improve their use of CSR practices when their teachers provide guided instruction that matches their learning needs. Collecting data on how individual students are doing and basing instructional decisions on these data make it more likely that students will get appropriate support. Think about what you expect most students to be able to do based on what you have taught, for example, identifying clunks and using fix-up strategies to figure out the clunks. Then determine which students are successfully able to implement the practice and which ones would benefit from additional support. This progress monitoring is not just for students with reading difficulties but for all students to ensure that everyone is stretching to apply reading comprehension strategies to increasingly more complex text. Provide opportunities to review and practice all strategies as you progress through teaching CSR.

Frequently Asked Questions About Progress Monitoring During CSR

When should I administer a progress-monitoring check?

Progress-monitoring checks should be administered after teaching students a strategy and engaging them in guided practice. Teachers who have used progress-monitoring procedures in the past have administered a check after they teach fix-up strategies one and two, fix-up strategies three and four, Get the Gist, and after each type of question generated during Wrap Up. Progress-monitoring checks can also be used at periodic times during the year.

What is the purpose of progress monitoring?

The purpose of progress monitoring is to determine what students know about a particular CSR strategy and how well they can apply it when reading. This information helps the teacher figure out what needs to be done to increase learning.

How long should progress-monitoring checks take?

Progress monitoring can typically be done with relatively few items and in a brief period of time (from five to fifteen minutes, depending on how many checks are included and how long they are). We provided one example already (for Right-There questions) and include other examples later in this chapter.

What does a progress-monitoring check look like?

To determine if students are successfully able to use one of the CSR strategies, for example, Get the Gist, we recommend providing them with one or two short paragraphs followed by explicit instructions to use the strategy.

Do students complete progress-monitoring checks in their CSR groups or individually?

Students complete progress-monitoring checks individually. These checks are part of the individual accountability that is so important for the success of CSR. They provide teachers with information on what students can do when working independently.

How do I decide whether to reteach the whole class or a subgroup of students who need guided practice?

If more than half of a class is struggling a great deal with a strategy, we suggest providing additional instruction with feedback for the entire class as the best approach. If everyone has some understanding, but some students need additional practice, consider a whole-class activity in which students practice the skill—something similar to the Gist Challenge at the end of this chapter. If you have a group of five or fewer students who do not understand how to engage in a CSR strategy, you could conduct small-group instruction.

Providing Additional Instruction

Students who struggle learning the CSR strategies may require additional instruction from the teacher. This may take the form of repeated teacher modeling or carefully planned guided practice. Following, you will learn some techniques that have been successful in the past in addressing students' difficulties with CSR strategies.

Targeted Instruction

After identifying small groups of struggling students, it is important to spend time planning targeted instruction that directly addresses areas of difficulty. For example, if a progress-monitoring check indicates that students are not writing strong gist statements, do not spend time reviewing the CSR previewing strategies. Instead, focus directly on writing high-quality gist statements. One way to help remain focused on targeted instruction is to write or use minilessons. Exhibit 4.1 will help students develop their ability to make evidence-based predictions. Exhibit 4.2 is a minilesson to help students identify well-written gists. Exhibit 4.3 gives additional practice in identifying well-written gists and helps students learn how to write them. Exhibit 4.4 is an example of a minilesson that may be used to aid students in Question Generation. Exhibit 4.5 helps students to learn to write Right-There and Author-and-You questions using pictures. Form 4.1 provides a question challenge game for students to increase the question-writing skills.

EXHIBIT 4.1. Evidence-Based Predictions

Objective: Students will identify information from the text that justifies their predictions.

Preparation: Draw a T-chart on the board or on a piece of paper. Entitle the left column "Prediction." Entitle the right column "Evidence."

- Explain to students that predictions are not simple guesses. They are informed guesses. Several sources can inform the predictions. They include titles, pictures, headings, and captions.

- Preview a short passage together drawing student attention to the title, pictures, headings, and captions.

- Systematically move through the previewed information to form predictions and record them on the T-chart. For example, you might say, "Let's look at the title. It says 'Creatures of the Deep.' What kinds of creatures does that title bring to your mind (fish, starfish, sharks, etc.)? Based on the title, what do you think you will learn about (sharks)?"

- Write "Sharks" in the prediction column. Remind students that they used the title to make their prediction, so write something like "The title says 'Creatures from the Deep' in the evidence column."

- Continue modeling using other sources (e.g., pictures, headings, and captions) and allow students to contribute as often as possible.

- You may choose to send a T-chart and a passage for homework practice in making evidence-based predictions.

EXHIBIT 4.2. Gist Minilesson

Objective: Students will identify well-written gist statements. They will also identify ways to improve poorly written gist statements.

Preparation: Identify several short paragraphs and write a gist statement for each one. The quality of the gist statements should vary. Prepare some poorly written statements, some moderately written statements, and some well-written statements.

- Review the qualities of well-written gists:
  - Complete sentence
  - Short sentence of about ten words
  - Contains the most important subject of the paragraph
  - Contains the most important information about the subject in the paragraph
  - Avoids minute details
- Explain that students will be reading several short paragraphs and gist statements. They will be responsible for identifying the quality of the gist and improving poorly written gist statements.
- Students read the first paragraph.
- Post the accompanying gist and lead students in a short evaluation of the gist. Is it a high-quality gist? If so, what makes it high quality? If not, how can it be improved?
- If the gist is of low quality, have students rewrite the gist (with or without your guidance as necessary).

EXHIBIT 4.3. Gist Challenge

Objective: To help students produce and recognize high-quality gists.

Use this lesson to reinforce gist writing and to increase the quality of students' gists. If time is limited, you may focus only on gists for this lesson and skip other CSR components. If you have more time, use this to focus on gists as a whole-class Wrap Up.

In this activity, student groups try to "out gist" each other.

- Provide a short reading divided into three sections. Share with the students that the focus for the day is to write high-quality gists that contain

(Continued)

- - The most important who or what
  - The most important information about the who or what
  - A complete sentence that is about ten words or less

- Groups read a section.

- Then, each group member writes his or her own gist for the section. The group agrees on the best gist or revises to have one super gist. Groups should discuss which gists are of high quality and why. When all sections are complete, the class comes back together to take the gist challenge. [You may also stop between sections and review gists instead of waiting until the end of class.]

- Teacher calls on one group randomly to share their gist and writes it on the board. The other groups are given the chance to challenge the first group's gist.

  - Teacher reads group one's gist.
    - Other groups are given thirty seconds to decide if they accept or challenge the gist.
    - If the groups accept the gist they must say what makes it a strong gist. If they accept the gist and it is determined to be an inadequate gist, the groups get no points. Groups are then given another chance to challenge.
    - If a group challenges the gist, they must provide another gist and a rationale for why their gist is better. More than one group can offer a challenge gist. The teacher is the judge. If a challenge gist is better and is a strong gist, move on to the next section. If the gist is not better, then groups are given a chance to rework their gists.

- Repeat process with remaining sections.

- *Optional:* Award points to groups for writing or recognizing high-quality gists.

Note to teacher: Throughout the process, the teacher should be providing feedback to encourage a strong gist and to distinguish poor gists from strong gists. Students should be able to provide support for why a gist is strong or not. If using points, all groups with strong gists should be given points.

EXHIBIT 4.4. Question Generation Minilesson

Objective: Students will write high-quality questions of different types.

Use this lesson to reinforce Question Generation and to increase the quality of students' questions.

In this activity, students stop after short sections of text and write questions with stems that you provide.

- Provide a short reading divided into several sections.

- Tell students the goal for today is to write high-quality questions.

- Group students in pairs as student A or B.

- In their pairs, student A should read the first section aloud while student B follows along. If students finish reading before time is up, have student B read the passage aloud to student A.

- At the end of the section, provide students with a question type and a stem. For example, "Write a Right-There question that begins with *who.*"

- Everyone writes a question. As students write questions, notice whose questions are of high quality.

- Choose one or two high-quality questions to share. First, ask the student to read the question aloud. Other students should be asked to provide the answer. Tell students why the question is of high quality (e.g., the answer can be found in the text; the question asks about important information you'll want to remember).

- Ask students to revise their questions if necessary.

- Repeat the procedure.

Notes to teacher:

- If your group of students struggles to a great extent with the skill, add teacher modeling to the beginning of this lesson.

- Throughout this process, the teacher should provide students with feedback to encourage questions that focus on important ideas to remember from the text.

EXHIBIT 4.5. Generating Questions Without Text

Objective: Students will learn to write Right-There and Author-and-You questions using pictures.

Preparation: Find three to four pictures or photos that prompt several questions. Pictures that convey action (e.g., sports scenes, nature scenes with animal action) usually work best.

The lesson today will help you learn how to write questions. We ask questions about almost everything we see. You write Right-There questions even when looking at the picture.

- Show the picture and discuss what is happening in the picture.

- Ask students, "What do you want to remember from this picture?" This becomes the answer to your question.

- Model for students how to write the question.

- You can use the same procedure for writing Author-and-You questions. Remind students to start Author-and-You questions with *why* or *how*. You can prompt them to think, "What do I wonder about this picture?"

- Model a few times with the small group.

- Then, give each student a different picture. Ask them to write a Right-There or Author-and-You question and then share it with the group. Have other group members provide the answer.

FORM 4.1. CSR Question Challenge

Name _____ **Date** _____

1. The teacher will ask you a question.

2. Discuss with your group the answer to the question.

3. Write your answer and be prepared to share with the class.

4. If your answer is correct, write in the number of points you earned.

OUR GROUP'S ANSWER	POINTS AWARDED
TOTAL	

High-Quality Feedback

A powerful way to identify and remediate difficulties students may face with CSR strategies is through the use of correction and feedback. In fact, high-quality feedback—when the teacher provides students with information about their performance—has a more powerful effect on student achievement than students' prior ability, socioeconomic status, or homework.[1] Although there are many forms of feedback, one of the most effective types is task-level feedback, when the teacher gives students information about their answer, behavior, understanding, or interpretation of the material.

One should formulate feedback according to three questions:[2]

- Where am I going?
- How am I doing?
- Where to next?

Consider Mrs. Clark once again. Mrs. Clark circulates around the room while students work independently to write a gist statement. She notices that Anna has a five-word sentence that contains the most important subject of the paragraph and one detail. Mrs. Clark stops Anna and says, "I see that you are writing a gist statement. Remember that a gist statement identifies the most important subject and then the most important information about the subject (Where am I going?). You have identified the correct subject, but you have written an interesting detail about him (How am I doing?). Instead, you need to find the most important information about him. I want you to reread these two sentences. Identify the most important thing about the subject and rewrite your gist statement (Where to next?). I will be back in two minutes to check on you." Table 4.1 shows some additional examples of high-quality, task-level feedback.

Learning Logs

Teachers can get a good sense for how their students are progressing with CSR by analyzing their learning logs.[3] We offer a CSR scoring rubric to help with this process in Form 4.2. Using a rubric enables teachers to evaluate students' proficiency with each strategy and to identify individual and common areas of confusion or error. We also provide additional suggestions for instruction based on data gleaned from learning logs. Learning logs can be found in Appendix A.

TABLE 4.1. Examples of High-Quality, Task-Level Feedback

FEEDBACK THAT ADDRESSES . . .	WHERE AM I GOING?	HOW AM I DOING?	WHERE TO NEXT?
Student behavior	*Remember, it is important that all group members contribute to the discussion during CSR time.*	*I have noticed that a couple of group members have not been given the opportunity to contribute.*	*During the next section of text, I want every group member to provide information that helps the group write a gist statement.*
Student understanding	*I can see that you are writing a Right-There question, so the answer has to be right in the text.*	*From the first paragraph, you ask, "How did lightning cause buildings to catch on fire?" Show me where in the text you found the answer* [can't be answered by the passage].	*There is some interesting information in these two sentences. Reread these sentences and underline something interesting. Write a question that goes with what you underline.*

FORM 4.2. CSR Scoring Rubric

Name _____ **Date** _____

Passage_____

	PROFICIENT 3	BECOMING PROFICIENT 2	NOT PROFICIENT 1	SCORE
Before				
Brainstorm	• Brainstorm is directly related to the topic.	• Brainstorm is somewhat related to the topic.	• Brainstorm is not at all related to the topic. • Text appears to be copied.	
Predict	• Clear use of topic, title, subheadings, and pictures to formulate prediction. • Relates well to text.	• Prediction is derived only from brainstorm. • Does not appear to relate well to text or topic.	• No evidence of use of passage topic, characteristics, or brainstorm in formulating prediction.	
During				
ID clunks	• Appropriate clunks selected—common rather than proper nouns.	• Limited evidence of self-monitoring: clunks are not identified by student (by teacher or book). • Clunks are words student already knows.	• No clunks listed when they are expected.	
Use fix-up strategies	• Use of any of four fix-up strategies to find the meaning of the clunk. • Brief definition is given.	• Does not use fix-up strategies correctly. • Asks the teacher instead of using fix-up strategy and working with group.	• Lists clunk with no definition. • Uses a dictionary before attempting a fix-up strategy.	
Get the Gist	• Names who or what and most important information of who or what. • Gist captures overall idea of section. • Gist is paraphrased and is approximately ten words. • Gist is a complete sentence.	• Names who or what but focuses on details rather than the main idea. • Part of gist may be copied from the text. • Gist is a complete sentence. • Gist may be very long.	• Incorrectly names who or what and focuses on details rather than the main idea. • Gist may be copied exactly from the text. • Gist is an incomplete sentence.	

FORM 4.2. (continued)

	PROFICIENT 3	BECOMING PROFICIENT 2	NOT PROFICIENT 1	SCORE
After				
Generate, ask, and answer questions	• More than one question type is used. • Important ideas from the text are captured in the questions. • Questions are written in question format. • Answers to questions can be found by looking in the text. • Answers are written in learning log.	• More than one question type is used. • Important ideas are inconsistently captured in the questions. • Lacks most important ideas. • Answers to questions can be found by looking in the text. • Answers are written in the learning log.	• Only one question type is given when more are expected. • Important ideas are not captured in the questions. • Questions are written as statements. • Questions are not related to the text. • Answers are not provided.	
Review	• Statement reflects important information. • Brief but complete sentence(s). • Review is paraphrased.	• Reflects important information but is detail focused.	• Lacks important information. • Detail focused. • Possibly copied from the text.	

Rubric scores can be used in several ways. Some teachers assign grades according to rubric scores. A perfect score on the rubric would be 21. So, 21 = 100 percent, 18 = 90 percent, 16 = 80 percent, and 14 = 70 percent. Other teachers use the rubric more holistically to identify individual student's strengths and weaknesses. It is possible that a student may have a good grasp of how to make a prediction and use the fix-up strategies—earning scores of 2 or 3—but still struggle with Get the Gist—earning a score of 1. With this type of data, teachers can identify students who may need to participate in minilessons that target specific strategies.

Comments:

TOTAL:

Addressing Common Student Errors

Students can make a variety of errors when engaging in any of the CSR strategies. In working with teachers and students across the nation, there are several errors that we have found to be common while learning to engage in these strategies. The following sections highlight some of the most common student errors and ways teachers may provide correction.

Brainstorm Errors

Brainstorm and prediction statements are the same. Teachers have reported that previewing is the easiest CSR component to teach. Yet when they analyze students' learning logs, teachers are surprised to find that their students are confusing brainstorm statements and predictions. Rather than brainstorming what they already know about a topic, they say what they believe an article will be about.

When students write predictions instead of brainstorms, it is important to be explicit about the differences in these two types of statements. A teacher might provide a few examples of prepared brainstorm statements and prediction statements and plan an activity in which the students must distinguish between the two. To gain a deep understanding of any reading strategy, students need to understand not only how to perform the component, but also why it is important. Students who understand the importance of brainstorming and why they are using this strategy are more likely to brainstorm correctly.

Brainstorms are too vague. Many times it is difficult to get a sense of what prior knowledge a student is accessing because it is not evident from his or her learning log entry. For example, a student may write "Fabrics are involved" for the topic *earth-friendly fabrics*. Teachers can tell students that they need to be convincing about what they know about the topic. The various text features (title, subheadings, pictures, captions, and keywords) can all be used to stimulate prior knowledge or connections. When students' brainstorms are vague or reflect an incomplete thought, it is likely that they are having trouble accessing prior knowledge of the topic. During the few minutes when students are writing their brainstorms, teachers can facilitate the process by asking the whole class leading questions about facets of the topic with which they should be familiar. For example, "What do you already know about things that are *earth-friendly*? What do you know about fabrics?" or "Look at the subheading that says 'Made from Waste.' When things are made from waste, they are recycled. What do you already know about recycling?"

Prediction Errors

Predictions are based only on the title. Students may make superficial predictions based only on the title when they have not previewed the passage. Alert students to first look at the headings, pictures, captions, bold words, and other features that stand out in the text and to use that information to formulate their predictions. Tell them that they will gain much more insight into the content of the text if they look beyond the title, which will ultimately help them monitor their comprehension. Display the text using a document camera or through some other means. Spend five minutes of whole-group instruction time having a few student volunteers point to the place in the text that led them to their prediction. Another option is to do a similar activity in small groups. After each prediction is stated, the rest of the group members try to guess the place in the text that led to that particular prediction. For each activity, students are drawn back to the text to make predictions that are connected to the text.

Clunks and Fix-Up Strategies Errors

Students do not have any clunks. Sometimes students do not encounter any unknown words in a section of text. However, it is more likely that students leave the clunk box blank in their learning logs for other reasons, most commonly that they are not carefully monitoring their understanding while they read. To identify a clunk, students must be able to recognize that they have a breakdown in understanding. Especially during the preliminary stages of fix-up strategy instruction, it is helpful to ask students to find at least two or three clunks per section or even to have students use fix-up strategies for preselected clunks. This alleviates any discomfort students may have with admitting to their peers that they don't know a word. It also provides practice with using the strategies for those who may already know a word's meaning, as well as for those who may partially know a word's meaning. Students must learn what type of word becomes a clunk. For example, students might say they know the word *misappropriation*, but when asked to explain the meaning, they are unable to provide a definition or to understand the meaning of the sentence in which the word was used. Teachers can demonstrate the different levels of knowing a word so that students learn to apply fix-up strategies for words that they may be familiar with but unclear about their definition in the text.

It can be difficult to gain insight into clunk fix-up strategy usage solely from the learning logs. Group observations and asking questions of individual students are also essential for assessing these skills.

Gist Errors

Gist is detail focused. Learning how to synthesize detailed information into a larger, more global idea can be difficult for many students. When planning gist lessons, especially in the early stages of gist instruction, it is helpful to use text that is conducive to locating a main idea. Before asking students to generate a gist statement, the teacher might try writing one herself. If the section doesn't lend itself to a gist statement (e.g., the paragraph is simply a list of factual information), a different paragraph or piece of text may be needed for instructional purposes.

Teachers might consider presenting a minilesson that aims to "prove" one gist as better than another. With a section of text projected for students to see, a teacher can present two or three prepared gists and assign different colors to each gist. Then she can highlight sections of the text that support each gist. Students should visually see that the color that is most prevalent represents the best gist.

Gist lacks important information. Many students begin their gists by writing "It's about how . . ." They likely begin this way because they are answering the question in their minds, "What is the section mostly about?"; however, such an answer typically leads to an incomplete gist. In this case, it is important to emphasize the need for a gist to be composed of two parts: (1) the most important who or what and (2) the most important thing about the who or what. Students first need practice with writing simple sentences that begin with the most important who or what (the subject) and end with the most important thing about the who or what (the predicate) before writing gists with more complex sentence structures. Gists should always be written in a complete sentence. Some teachers ask students to agree in their small groups on the most important who or what in the passage before going on to write their individuals gists. This way, students work together and have some prediscussion about the section's meaning before working on their gist statements.

Another reason for incomplete gists is an overemphasis on word count. Students may first need very flexible word count limits (five to fifteen) before implementing more stringent limits (eight to twelve).

Question Generation Errors

Questions are not varied. Students first need to understand the differences between question types before being able to write varied questions. If students are only writing Right-There questions when they have been asked to write different types of questions, then it is likely that they need further instruction on other types of questions. In the same way, students who always begin a question the same way (e.g. "What is a . . . ?") can be encouraged to use other question stems and be provided with additional instruction as needed.

Questions lack important information. Questions should focus on important information that was learned from the text. Other CSR strategies may be helpful in determining important information, especially the gist strategy. Looking back to the gists can help with question writing; generating gists garner similar synthesis skills as those used to generate higher-level, teacher-type questions. As students begin to develop their understanding of questions, it may be helpful for them to write their gist as a question. The words *how* and *why* are generally good sentence starters for higher-level questions. Once students are familiar with question writing, they can move away from using gist statements and write more creative, original questions.

Answers to questions cannot be found in the text. It is fairly common for students to write questions that require additional sources of information to answer. Although these questions may be interesting and thought provoking, they do not usually facilitate comprehension of the information presented in the passage itself. Teachers can remind students that the purpose of writing and answering questions in CSR is to help them understand and remember what they have read. For this reason, questions should stay with the text. After students write their questions, they can highlight the places in the text where the information can be found to answer each question. By highlighting the text and writing answers to their own questions, students will become aware of questions that may need to be revised. Questions that go beyond the text can be saved for use in follow-up activities.

Review Errors

Review reflects only information gained from a Preview. The purpose of review is to identify the critical information across a large section of text. A review that reflects information gained from the Preview is not incorrect; it is likely just incomplete. Similar to previously mentioned activities, students can practice locating the sources of information in their reviews by highlighting, circling, pointing, or talking with others. They can be made aware that in doing so, they are demonstrating more in-depth comprehension. A key component of the review strategy is to have students provide evidence for why their review statements reflect the most important information in the text.

Review is a "fun fact." It is important to celebrate with students when they find information from their reading that is interesting or fun. Although a review statement is intended to help students create overall meaning from the passage, students should not feel discouraged from writing fun facts. They can write two review statements, one that captures the big ideas and one that reflects merely interesting information. However, if students write both statements, they should be able to say which contains the most important ideas and which contains the fun fact.

Review statements are incorrect. If students are misunderstanding the general content of the passage, then it is likely they are struggling to effectively use the other CSR strategies. A teacher may need to review the previous sections of the learning log and determine if other strategies need attention in conjunction with the review.

Student learning logs are a rich source of information that provide teachers with insight into students' understanding of the CSR strategies. When only one or a small group of students is struggling with a strategy, teachers can target individual or small-group focus lessons to provide additional support. When teachers recognize common areas in need of attention, they can use this information to plan for the class in ways that will deepen students' reading skills, providing students with access to broader scopes of literature.

Conclusion

There are many ways to collect data about students' progress. In this chapter, we have highlighted just a couple, progress-monitoring checks and learning logs. Yet, effective teachers keep tabs on their students' progress in multiple ways. In CSR, teachers collect data when they listen in on "kidtalk" as students work in their cooperative groups. They also examine unit tests to make sure students are meeting standards and learning sufficient content. Data from all of these sources can be used to plan differentiated instruction.

Part III

Providing CSR Professional Development and Ongoing Support

CHAPTER 5

Providing CSR Professional Development

> "You have worked out all the kinks. Reciprocal Teaching, as great as it is, just seemed too challenging to implement with an entire class. But you've figured out how to make it work. I love it. If the superintendent were to say that starting tomorrow every teacher in M-DCPS would have to implement CSR in order to keep their job in this district, I would jump up and down and shout "hallelujah!"

—THE MIAMI-DADE COUNTY PUBLIC SCHOOLS [M-DCPS]
LANGUAGE ARTS DIRECTOR

> "I really support CSR. I have always made my best effort to present programs and pilots to kids, but this is the first one that has the potential for lasting impact. I place my entire educational philosophy into the realm of creating lifelong and independent learners, and CSR is a program that seems truly aligned with this philosophy."

—MIDDLE SCHOOL SOCIAL STUDIES TEACHER

> "[When asked which students benefited the most from CSR:] Um, I think, really, they all benefited, because they're all at different levels, and so they used the strategies in different ways. Like, students at different levels used the clunk strategies in different ways. That helped the lower-level students really comprehend what they were reading a lot more. And then, it helped the higher-level students really go deep into those words and have great discussions about the meaning of words. . . . CSR generated a lot of great discussion in their groups."

—MIDDLE SCHOOL LANGUAGE ARTS TEACHER

What is an ambitious but noteworthy goal for effective CSR professional development (PD)? We hope that teachers will expand their understanding of reading comprehension strategy instruction, integrate CSR into their existing curriculum and practice, and maintain their implementation of CSR over time. Through ongoing professional development that relates to the classroom context, CSR becomes part of a teacher's repertoire of what works in the classroom. Effective professional development accomplishes the following:[1]

- Focuses on teaching-specific content (e.g., CSR PD situates reading comprehension instruction into teachers' content area)

- Provides opportunities for active learning (e.g., throughout PD, teachers engage in activities that allow them to be the student as they learn the strategies for themselves and to be the teacher as they plan and reflect on their role)

- Offers information that is aligned with personal beliefs as well as school and district initiatives (e.g., teachers connect what they are learning to what they are currently teaching; PD providers work with district and content coordinators to align CSR instruction with curriculum)

- Is sufficient in duration (CSR PD ideally continues throughout the school year; as teachers deepen their understanding they are given chances to refine their practice and reflection through follow-up booster sessions)

- Includes collective participation (e.g., teachers from the same grade level, department, or school are encouraged to attend together)

Professional development in CSR generally includes setting the purpose for reading comprehension, learning the CSR strategies and how they fit together, introducing and managing cooperative learning, and fine-tuning implementation. These components can be spread out over time throughout the school year or as we recommend here, provided with a two-day initial professional development session, followed by several sessions that we refer to as "booster" sessions (see Figure 5.1).

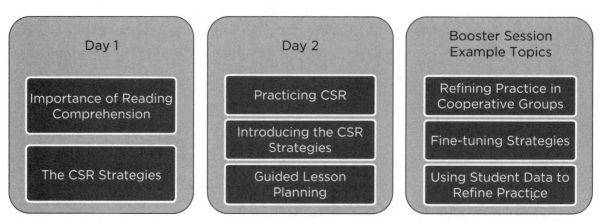

FIGURE 5.1. Professional Development

Introducing Reading Comprehension Strategy Instruction

During the initial professional development, introduce teachers to comprehension strategy instruction and provide them with statistics that make the case for its value in classrooms. This initial section of PD takes approximately forty-five minutes. If possible, add local figures that represent the population of students your teachers have in their classrooms to increase the relevance of these data. If CSR will be taught in content area classrooms such as social studies and science, it is also important to set the stage for why reading instruction should occur outside of reading and language arts and to include explicit alignment with curriculum goals.

When we provide PD, we use a series of PowerPoint slides. Here we present the basic information from these slides as exhibits. All the exhibits in this chapter can be downloaded as PowerPoint slides for free from www.josseybass.com/go/csr. You might want to add pictures or other visuals to the slides to personalize them.

Teachers benefit from a clear explanation and activity that defines reading comprehension strategy instruction (Exhibit 5.1). We use a vignette that presents a reading lesson on *Eleven* by Sandra Cisneros in which a teacher provides seemingly adequate typical instruction.[2] The teacher in the vignette helps her students to understand the text by asking comprehension questions, clarifying students' understanding, and summarizing students' responses. We ask participants in the CSR PD to consider the instruction, how it supports students' learning, and in what areas it can be improved.

EXHIBIT 5.1. The Importance of Comprehension Strategies Instruction

Why Do We Need to Teach Reading Across the Content Areas?

- As students progress through school, the emphasis moves from learning to read to reading to learn.

- Significant numbers of adolescents do not adequately understand complex texts, impeding their success in school, access to postsecondary learning, and opportunities within a competitive work environment.[3]

- Forty-one states reported that only 18.7 percent of ELLs scored above state-established norms for reading comprehension.[4]

- The readability level of some texts used in secondary classrooms may be too high for below-grade-level readers and the "unfriendliness" of some texts can result in comprehension challenges for many students.[5]

The second part of the *Eleven* vignette includes a debriefing session with the observer of the lesson (and author of the vignette). The observer helps the teacher see that although students may have left class understanding the content of the specific text read in class, the teacher did not provide the students with any skills that would transfer and help them understand *other* texts. In other words, the teacher did not teach them reading comprehension strategies that could help them make sense of future readings.[6] Students require explicit instruction in reading comprehension strategies so that they have tools to understand and remember what they read on their own. CSR provides a model to teach those important reading strategies.

Connecting CSR to Reading in the Classroom

Next, we ask teachers about reading in their own classrooms. We suggest using a think-pair-share or table share to allow teachers to discuss the questions in Exhibit 5.2. The purpose of this activity is to orient teachers toward reading comprehension strategy instruction and situate that knowledge into the types of teaching and learning activities they already use in their own classrooms.

Overview of CSR

After this introduction, teachers are ready to learn about CSR. Exhibits 5.3 through 5.5 provide teachers with an overview of CSR and include information about the importance of cooperative learning. Use the CSR Plan for Strategic Reading (Figure 1.1) to illustrate briefly the CSR strategies and how they fit together within a reading lesson. This portion of PD takes about thirty minutes.

EXHIBIT 5.2. Connecting to Your Classroom

What Does Reading Look Like in Your Classroom?

- What types of reading activities do you use in your classroom?
- In what ways do students read (teacher read aloud, silent reading, round robin, cooperative learning)?
- What do you like about reading activities in your class and what are some of the challenges for your students (e.g., ELLs, students with disabilities, high achievers)?

EXHIBIT 5.3. The Importance of CSR

CSR addresses multiple challenges in the classroom:

- How to teach text-comprehension strategies to students

- How to promote students' reading comprehension, particularly of discipline-specific expository text

- How to help ELLs, students with LD, and struggling readers access grade-level content and support their text-based content learning

- How to increase student engagement in high-level academic discussions

- How to support ELLs' language acquisition through academic discourse with peers

EXHIBIT 5.4. What Is Collaborative Strategic Reading?

- Collaborative Strategic Reading (CSR) combines reading comprehension strategy instruction[7] and cooperative learning.[8]

- In CSR, students read and discuss text through a combination of teacher-led activities and student-led cooperative group work.

- CSR promotes content learning, language acquisition, and reading comprehension in diverse classrooms that include English language learners and students with learning disabilities.[9]

EXHIBIT 5.5. Why Is Cooperative Learning an Important Part of CSR?

Cooperative learning can

- Increase academic performance, motivation, engagement, time on task, self-esteem, and positive social behaviors

- Foster the development of higher-order thinking skills

- Facilitate the integration of culturally and linguistically diverse learners and learners of a wide range of achievement levels, including students with special needs

- Provide opportunities to interact and discuss and have learning scaffolded

- Be most effective when all group members have an assigned, meaningful task[10]

Many teachers appreciate knowing that the new practices they are learning about in PD are supported by research. You may want to include information summarizing the CSR research studies that are provided in Appendix B or assign Appendix B for teachers to read before or during the PD.

Learning the CSR Strategies

We divide CSR professional development into learning the CSR strategies and teaching CSR to your students. The CSR strategies are not difficult to learn and many teachers are already familiar with using some before-, during-, and after-reading strategies. But, to teach CSR well, teachers have to spend sufficient time learning it and teaching it to their students. It takes time to go over each strategy with students and provide them with multiple opportunities to practice. Similar to when teachers introduce the CSR strategies to their students, when we introduce each strategy during PD, we provide support by asking the following questions:

- What is the strategy?
- Why is it important?
- When is it used?
- How do students use the strategy?

For each strategy, we suggest offering several examples as well as practice activities. Examples should include the variety of content areas represented by the teachers in the PD. For instance, if sixth-grade science teachers attend the PD, then some activities should reflect readings from the local science curriculum used by those teachers. Although timing may vary, forty-five to sixty minutes should be reserved for each strategy.

Teachers also practice using the CSR materials during PD, particularly the CSR learning log, the teacher cue cards, and the lesson planning template (see Appendix A for these CSR materials). We recommend that you introduce these first and then have copies available for teachers to use.

Preview

Exhibit 5.6 outlines the preview strategy for use during PD. These steps are the same as those explained in the Preview section of Chapter Two, "Teaching the CSR Strategies to Students."

We suggest that you tell participants that Preview is always teacher led and occurs one time before reading. Preview sets the stage for reading and helps teachers connect CSR to the curriculum or other units of study. It is brief, five to seven minutes, and allows students to access prior knowledge about a topic and for teachers to build

EXHIBIT 5.6. What Is CSR Preview?

- Teacher states the topic.

- Teacher presents important vocabulary and concepts using pictures, charts, graphic organizers, short videos, and brief descriptions (two to three).

- Students preview the text (read headings, subheadings, bold words, charts, etc.).

- Students brainstorm and write what they already know about the topic in their learning logs. Students share briefly with their partner or group. Teacher builds background knowledge using pictures, charts, graphic organizers, short videos, and brief descriptions.

- Students write predictions. Students share briefly with their partner or group. Teacher provides feedback.

- Teacher states the purpose for reading.

background knowledge that is needed to understand the text. Exhibit 5.7 explains why Preview is important for student learning.

Teachers learn to teach Preview with three activities. First, the presenter models how to use the strategy. Next, teachers work in groups of three or four to plan the Preview portion of a lesson using a reading from their curriculum or from sample texts provided in PD. Finally, one of the group members practices leading the Preview portion of a lesson while others in the small group assume the student roles. The CSR Scoring Rubric (Form 4.2) can be used as a guide to provide feedback.

To model Preview, use a textbook or supplemental reading from the local curriculum to walk teachers through the steps. Include pictures or a short video clip to preteach vocabulary or key ideas. Use a timer to model how the teacher can keep the lesson moving and still allow students time to write on their own and to share. In Preview, point out the parts that are introduced by the teacher and also how students will use their learning logs to write down their own brainstorms and predictions. Students always share their ideas with a partner or their small group. As the presenter models Preview, he or she is the teacher and the participants become the students to simulate how CSR looks and feels in a real classroom. Participants will need a blank learning log they can use to practice each strategy.

In small groups, participants use the strategy guide and the CSR Lesson-Planning Template (Form 5.1) to practice planning the Preview portion of a lesson. Teachers consider words and concepts to preteach, questions to ask to guide the brainstorm section, and connections to the curriculum. In each small group, one partner is the

---

EXHIBIT 5.7. Why Is Preview Important?

Preteaching Key Vocabulary

- Provides explicit instruction with visuals and other tools to contextualize learning and make it comprehensible

- Increases the number of times and the different ways students learn about key terms

- Draws attention to important ideas essential for understanding the text

- Clarifies words that might be confusing, especially for ELLs, such as words with multiple meanings

Brainstorming to Access Background Knowledge

- Activates schema that aids understanding, interest, and memory

- Helps students make connections with prior learning

- Alerts the teacher to students' misconceptions

Building Background Knowledge

- Enhances students' knowledge of the topic and helps to create a relevant schema

- Creates a shared understanding among the students in a class

---

teacher and practices presenting the Preview portion of the CSR lesson using explicit directions, explanations, and the timer to monitor response time. The other group members assume the role of students. After the practice session, the group debriefs and completes the notes section of the strategy guide. Many participants find it helpful to switch roles and to repeat the practice to fine-tune the delivery of Preview.

After teachers have practiced the Preview process, allow them to take on the role of the teacher to plan how Preview can be used in a classroom. Using materials from their own classroom (e.g., a textbook or supplemental reading) or a practice reading provided at PD, offer time for teachers to plan the Preview by using the CSR Lesson-Planning Template, which will be used throughout the PD. Teachers consider words and concepts to preteach, questions to ask to guide the brainstorm section, and connections to the curriculum. Participants use the teacher cue cards to plan their Preview (see Appendix A). Allow time for participants to debrief the planning process.

Teachers can avoid common mistakes by being prepared. Students who are unfamiliar with a topic or not accustomed to participating may shut down during brainstorming if they are not able to make a quick connection to the topic (see

FORM 5.1. CSR Lesson-Planning Template

Teacher:	Content area:	Grade:

Lesson outcomes:

Reading topic:

BEFORE Reading

Brainstorm: Connections to background knowledge:

Additional info for students:	Visuals/Video/Realia
Words and concepts to preteach (two to three): 1. 2. 3.	

Students preview passage: Look at the headings, subheadings, pictures, and so on to preview the text.

Prediction: Based on your preview of this passage, what do you think you will learn in this text? Purpose for reading:

DURING Reading
Section One

Possible clunks:

Scaffolding the student gists Most important who or what: Most important things about the who or what:	Possible gist(s)

Section Two

Possible clunks:

Most important who or what: Most important things about the who or what:	Possible gist(s)

Section Three

Possible clunks:

Most important who or what: Most important things about the who or what:	Possible gist(s)

AFTER Reading

Possible questions:

Possible review statement(s):

Whole-Class Teacher-Led Wrap Up

Important points and connections: Strategy review, as needed (e.g., review strategies used to find clunk, gists, etc.):

EXHIBIT 5.8. Avoid the Pitfalls: Preview

If students say they can't write their brainstorm:

- Widen the lens by asking questions about related information they are likely to know (e.g., clouds and cloud types in general rather than one specific type of clouds, such as cumulus)

- Build background knowledge

- Make explicit connections to prior knowledge and other units of study

---

EXHIBIT 5.9. Recap: Teacher's Role During Preview

- Help students access relevant background knowledge and make connections with previous learning and their everyday lives.

- Build background knowledge important for understanding content.

- Consider leading a more in-depth Preview at the beginning of a new unit or long reading.

- Introduce two to three key vocabulary terms.

- Ask students to share their ideas with a partner or in their CSR small groups after brainstorming and predicting.

- Monitor closely and provide feedback as needed when students brainstorm and predict.

- Provide time for students to share their brainstorms and predictions with a partner or small group.

- Set the purpose for reading by summarizing key ideas students mention in their predictions.

Exhibit 5.8). In this case, the teacher's role is to help students find ways to connect what they are learning. This can be done by expanding the brainstorm to a more accessible topic (for example, from what you know about sustainable development to what you know about ways we recycle), by building background knowledge, and by making explicit connections to what students know or have already learned. Demonstrations, short video clips, pictures, maps, and other visuals can support students in connecting to what they already know about a topic and in piquing their interest to learn more.

Before moving on to the next strategy, Click and Clunk, provide a quick recap and ask teachers to reflect on how Preview is similar to and different from what they currently do in the classroom. Exhibit 5.9 can be used to review the purpose of the Preview strategy.

EXHIBIT 5.10. What Is Click and Clunk?

- Click (cruise control):
    - When you understand what you read, everything "clicks" along smoothly.
- Clunk (traffic jam):
    - When you don't understand what you read—"clunk"—you stop. When you get to a clunk, use the fix-up strategies to figure out what the word or phrase means.

EXHIBIT 5.11. Why Is Click and Clunk Important?

- Monitoring understanding and identifying clunks is a metacognitive skill essential for comprehension.
- Click and Clunk helps students to be more active, engaged readers.
- Good readers use different strategies to figure out the meaning of words and difficult ideas while reading.
- Click and Clunk gives several ways to approach unfamiliar vocabulary, including the use of cognates for ELLs.

Click and Clunk

Exhibit 5.10 outlines Click and Clunk and its strategy.

In PD, we explain that Click and Clunk is a metacognitive strategy that helps students recognize when their understanding breaks down and gives them skills to fix up the misunderstanding. By using fix-up strategies, students learn to use context clues and word analysis skills to figure out the meaning of unknown words or concepts. Consider this example. A teacher is reading an article for a night class. While reading, her mind wanders and soon she is making a mental shopping list and planning how she might reorganize her reading groups. When she gets to the end of the page, she realizes she has no idea what she just read. A good reader will automatically refocus, reread, and figure out if other strategies are needed to repair the misunderstanding. Click and Clunk provides a structure that engages students in this same process. See Chapter Two for additional explanations of the Click and Clunk strategy to use during PD or with students.

We recommend that you present information about why Click and Clunk is important and then teach the strategies (see Exhibits 5.11 through 5.14). First introduce teachers to the steps of Click and Clunk and then provide opportunities to practice.

EXHIBIT 5.12. What Are the Steps for Click and Clunk?

1. After reading a section of text, stop and identify any words or ideas that you do not understand. Write your clunks in your learning log.

2. Work with your group to use fix-up strategies to figure out the meaning of the unknown words or ideas. Circle the strategy (or strategies) you use in your learning log.

EXHIBIT 5.13. What a Clunk Is and Is Not

- A clunk is
    - A word or concept you don't know how to define in the context of the reading
- A clunk is not
    - A proper noun

EXHIBIT 5.14. Clunk Fix-Up Strategies

- Reread the sentence with the clunk and look for key ideas to help you figure out the word. Think about what makes sense.
- Reread the sentences before and after the clunk, looking for clues.
- Break the word apart and look for word parts (prefixes, suffixes, root words) or smaller words you know.
- Look for a cognate that makes sense.

Exhibit 5.15 points out that clunks can be figured out using context clues. In the second example, the first sentence is not sufficient to figure out the meaning of the word *implore*. However, by reading the next sentence, the word is essentially defined. *Implore* means to beg or plead. Students learn that fix-up strategies one and two involve what some teachers call "reading around the word," whereas fix-up strategies three and four require students to look more closely at the word, or to "read within the word," looking for word parts they know or making a connection to a cognate in their first language.

EXHIBIT 5.15. Click and Clunk Examples: Context Clues: Fix-Up Strategies One and Two

- Mr. Marz asked James to rewrite his messy assignment because he could not **decipher** his handwriting. (strategy one)
- Mrs. Greenteacher **implored** her students to behave. Yet this begging and pleading were not enough. She needed high expectations, engaging assignments, and more structure in her class. (strategy two)

EXHIBIT 5.16. Click and Clunk Examples: Word Analysis: Fix-Up Strategy Three

- In the early days, gold was **transported** from the mines to nearby villages in wagons. (strategies one and three)

In Exhibit 5.16, the definition of a clunk is gained by analyzing the word. Transported includes the prefix *trans-*, meaning across, and the root *port*, meaning to carry. The suffix *-ed* indicates past tense. To check the meaning of the word, students reread the sentence, inserting the new definition. With the word *transported*, context clues and word parts contribute useful information about the word's meaning.

The use of fix-up strategy three is supported by additional instruction in prefixes, roots, and suffixes, skills many educators already teach. Making connections for students between word parts they have learned in class and the application of word parts in CSR is an effective way for students to transfer their learning. In addition, during CSR students have access to student resource materials (see Appendix A), with lists of these helpful word parts. At this point in the PD, show these lists to participants and point out that the word parts in *transported* are all found in the student resources. Teachers using CSR in content-area classrooms such as social studies or science often provide customized lists of high-frequency prefixes, suffixes, and root words that are content specific.

We recommend that you refer to Chapter Two for notes about cognates and review Exhibit 5.17. It is important for teachers to know the definition of a cognate, when a cognate might be useful, and for whom. A cognate is a word that looks the same *and* has the same meaning in more than one language. Although there are many useful cognates, ELLs do not always switch between their first language and English to use this strength. Thus, pointing out cognate use in fix-up strategies can help students add this skill to their strategy toolkit. There are also false cognates, which are words that look the same,

---

EXHIBIT 5.17. Using Fix-Up Strategy Four: Cognates

- Cognates are words in two languages that share a similar meaning.
- Thirty to 40 percent of words in English have a related word in Spanish.
- Lots of languages have cognates in English (e.g., Arabic).
- Teaching students to recognize cognates supports comprehension.
- Not all words that look the same have similar meanings. Always check for false cognates.
- Fix-up strategy four is used only with students who speak a language other than English.[11]

EXHIBIT 5.18. Click and Clunk Example: Cognates: Fix-Up Strategy Four

- It's important for students to **participate** during class. (strategy four)

---

but do not have the same meaning. For example, the word *embarrass* has a false Spanish cognate. Embarrass looks very much like the Spanish word, *embarazada*. However, the English translation of *embarazada* is pregnant. When students use cognates, they should always put the definition back into the sentence to check that it makes sense. Finally, note that cognates are only useful when students speak a language other than English. We have observed many students sharing their cognate knowledge with their English-only peers. Not only do all students benefit from the additional resource, but it is a way to value knowing two languages.

In Exhibit 5.18, the word *participate* has a cognate. The words look similar and share a common definition in Spanish (*participar*), in French (*participer*), and in other languages as well.

Once participants are familiar with the fix-up strategies, we suggest providing them with time to consider the clunks students might have in their classrooms. Draw on the same practice text that participants used to plan the Preview portion of the lesson and continue to complete the lesson-planning template (see Exhibit 5.19). Teachers should take some time to consider possible student clunks and how fix-up strategies could be used. Teachers will notice that not all words can be readily figured out with fix-up strategies and can consider how they will work with students to understand those words. An important component of the Click and Clunk strategy is that students learn to regulate their understanding and to identify words or concepts that they identify as

EXHIBIT 5.19. Click and Clunk: Lesson Planning Activity

- On your own, look through _____. Underline words that your students might identify as clunks and write them on the lesson-planning template.

- Discuss with a partner the fix-up strategy(ies) that could be used to figure out the meaning of each word.

- Words that would be difficult to figure out with a fix-up strategy.

EXHIBIT 5.20. Avoid the Pitfalls: "I Don't Have Any Clunks."

Occasionally students:

Don't think they have any clunks

- Sometimes students think they know a word because it sounds familiar. Help students understand that a clunk is a word you can't define.

- Sometimes students aren't reading carefully enough to find clunks. Help students practice finding clunks.

Don't want to look like they don't know

- Good readers have clunks. Model having your own clunks. Create a safe environment.

Just don't have any clunks . . .

- Check the reading level. Readings that are too easy or too difficult may yield few clunks.

clunks. Often students have clunks that are not on the teacher's list of possible clunks. In other words, planning a lesson by identifying possible clunks prepares the teachers to support students but does not preclude students from finding their own clunks during reading. It is important that students come up with their own clunks.

Next review Exhibit 5.20 with participants. These are common occurrences that coaches have observed in classrooms as teachers begin to implement CSR, with tips for how to support students in overcoming these challenges. There are a variety of reasons why students might not have clunks while reading.

Before moving on to the next strategy, Get the Gist, provide a quick recap and ask teachers to reflect on how Click and Clunk is similar to and different from what they currently do in the classroom. Teachers should also consider additional skills that will

EXHIBIT 5.21. Recap: The Teacher's Role During Click and Clunk

During CSR

- Support students to use all of the fix-up strategies. Students do not need to try the fix-up strategies in order but, for example, might jump right to number four if they recognize a cognate.

- Listen in on groups and check students' learning logs.

- Question students who don't have clunks; for example, "What does *noxious* mean? What is the meaning of *trigger* in this paragraph?"

- Ask students to explain how they got the definition for their clunks.

- Revisit common clunks.

- Ask students to share how they used fix-up strategies to find the meaning of a clunk.

Follow-Up Activities

- Ask students to do follow-up activities in class or as homework to reinforce important clunks.

- Provide additional instruction in prefixes, root words, suffixes, and cognates.

- Verify word meanings.

- Play word games (e.g., "Clunk Concentration").

- Add clunks to word walls with their definitions.

- Develop clunk graphic and semantic organizers.

Note: CSR is *not* a comprehensive vocabulary program. To learn words deeply, students require additional instruction and practice.

need to be taught, such as using cognates or providing additional instruction in word parts. Exhibit 5.21 can be used to review the teacher's role during the Click and Clunk strategy.

Get the Gist

Exhibits 5.22 through 5.24 outline the Get the Gist strategy.

EXHIBIT 5.22. What Is Get the Gist?

Get the Gist has three steps:

1. Name the who or what that the section is mostly about.

2. Identify the most important information about the who or what.

3. Write a gist statement in about ten words.

EXHIBIT 5.23. When Is Get the Gist Used?

- Get the Gist is used during reading.

- Students monitor their understanding and think about what is most important while reading.

- Students stop and find the meaning of their clunks and then figure out the gist at the end of each section of text.

EXHIBIT 5.24. Why Is Get the Gist Important?

- People do not remember everything they read.

- Good readers process individual ideas but remember just the most important parts—the main ideas of what they read (and perhaps some interesting details).

- During reading, strong readers
  - Implicitly generate a gist after each paragraph
  - Make inferences and connections between paragraphs[12]

Next, ask participants to practice using the Get the Gist strategy. Examples can be drawn from local curricula or higher-level reading passages, such as shown in Exhibits 5.25 and 5.26.

Participants now return to their lesson-planning template and their practice passage (see Exhibit 5.27). In this activity, teachers familiarize themselves with the Get the Gist strategy and also continue to follow a lesson-planning routine that will help them prepare for teaching. Teachers who prepare gists prior to the lesson are able to provide more specific feedback related to the quality of the gists students are writing.

EXHIBIT 5.25. Get the Gist Example: Noise Pollution

Noise pollution in oceans has risen dramatically because of an increase in commercial shipping, oil and gas prospecting, and other activities. Evidence is mounting that low-frequency noise from these and other sources can pulp delicate organs in squid, octopuses, and cuttlefish.[13]

EXHIBIT 5.26. Get the Gist Example: Practice

Who or What?

- Noise pollution

Important Information

- Noise pollution is occurring in oceans.
- Noise pollution is rising dramatically.
- Noise pollution is caused by commercial shipping, oil and gas prospecting, and other activities.
- Low-frequency noise from these activities may be harming ocean animals.

Gist

- Noise pollution from industrial activities is increasingly harming ocean animals.

EXHIBIT 5.27. Gist: Lesson-Planning Activity

- On your own, read _____. Stop after each section to identify a gist and write it in the lesson plan.
- Discuss with a partner:
  - Are your gists similar or different?
  - Is there more than one acceptable gist?

EXHIBIT 5.28. Avoid the Pitfalls: Gist

All gists in a group are exactly the same.

- First, have students agree on the most important who or what.

- Use a timer and provide silent work time for students to complete their gists independently (two to three minutes).

- Finally, have students discuss their gists.

Gists include details but not the most important information.

- Shorten the length of text used to create a gist.

- Practice distinguishing details from important information.

- Demonstrate visually (e.g., highlight in a passage) how a variety of information from a section is included in the gist.

Students don't discuss their gists.

- Show students that sharing (e.g., giving information) is not the same as discussing (e.g., providing evidence, asking questions, giving feedback).

- Spotlight a group or show a video of students having a high-quality discussion.

- Lead a whole-class discussion comparing several student gists.

Encourage teachers to share their gists with one another and to discuss the features of a high-quality gist.

After teachers have had some experience writing gists, review Exhibit 5.28 with participants. Encourage teachers to discuss challenges their students might have with Get the Gist and possible solutions.

Before moving on to Wrap Up, take some time to review the teacher's role during Get the Gist (see Exhibit 5.29). Point out that Get the Gist is a student-led activity that occurs during reading when students are in cooperative learning groups. The teacher's role is to monitor groups, provide feedback, and to bring the whole class together to reteach or highlight key points.

Wrap Up

Exhibit 5.30 outlines the Wrap Up strategy.

Wrap Up is shared by the teacher and students. In small groups, students write questions and answers and write a review statement or a short summary of what they learned. Students ask and answer each other's questions and share their review

---

EXHIBIT 5.29. Recap: Teacher's Role During Get the Gist

- Prepare gists for each section prior to the lesson.

- Check that students identify the most important who or what.

- Check whether students include the most important information (not just details).

- Check that students are writing their own gists.

- Encourage student-led small-group discussion. Students need to say why gists have the most important information using the text as evidence.

- Bring the group back together to reteach, highlight key points, or evaluate gists together as a class.

EXHIBIT 5.30. What Is Wrap Up?

Question Generation

- Think of questions and write them in your learning log.

- Write questions and answers.

- Ask and answer questions with your group.

Review

- Think about what you just read.

- Write the most important ideas from the passage.

- Share with your group, providing evidence to support your ideas.

- Teacher leads a whole-class Wrap Up.

---

statements with one another. Then, the teacher brings the students back together to do a whole-class Wrap Up of the reading. Exhibit 5.31 discusses when Wrap Up is used and Exhibit 5.32 describes its importance.

Question Generation

Using a short section of text, we suggest that you model different types of questions that students can generate. Some questions are factual and straightforward and others

---

EXHIBIT 5.31. When Is Wrap Up Used?

- Wrap Up occurs only once during a CSR lesson, after students have finished reading the day's text.

EXHIBIT 5.32. Why Is Wrap Up Important?

- Asking and answering questions helps students to
  - Identify main ideas
  - Summarize text
  - Monitor their understanding
  - Integrate information from different parts of the text
  - Apply higher-level thinking skills (e.g., making inferences)
  - Remember what they read
- Teaching students to review the most important information they learned helps them to remember what they have read.
- Asking students to justify their responses helps students to be more active, engaged readers and requires higher-level thinking.

---

require students to make inferences or connect what they have just learned with what they already know. Exhibit 5.33 models question writing.

Have teachers discuss the types of questions that are modeled in the example. Q1 is very straightforward and can be answered directly from the text. Q2 can be answered by reading the text, but allows students to go beyond the text to make connections. Q3 encourages students to relate the topic to their daily lives. Students should be encouraged to write questions at various levels. As noted in Chapter Two, using question words and question stems supports students to write questions.

Because question asking is often the teacher's domain, participants may benefit from a turn and talk to discuss the difference between teachers asking questions and students generating and asking questions (see Exhibit 5.34).

As teachers share their thinking, refer to Exhibit 5.32, highlighting the benefits of allowing students time to ask and answer their own questions about the text. First and foremost, generating questions requires students to go back to the text, reread, and think about what they learned. Students check their understanding and work to remember the important ideas as they figure out a good question. Students also practice standard structures for writing questions and answers and are motivated to write strong questions when they know they will share with their classmates.

EXHIBIT 5.33. Question Generation

Ben Franklin and Electricity

Have you ever seen what lightning can do when it strikes a building? It is so powerful that a strike can cause buildings and other structures to erupt in flames. During Ben Franklin's time, fires from lightning were a large concern for people. This is one reason he wanted to study lightning. Franklin was one of the greatest scientists of his time. Indeed, his work and experiments resulted in several important discoveries and inventions.

Ben Franklin was born in Boston, Massachusetts, on January 17, 1706. One of seventeen children, his father could afford to send him to school for only one year, so he went to work for his brother, a printer. While there, Ben read many books and taught himself to become a good writer. When he was seventeen, he ran away to Philadelphia, Pennsylvania, where he performed many of his science experiments. In addition, he helped draft, or write, the Constitution of the United States of America and, as a result, is known as one of this country's forefathers. He died in 1790 at the age of eighty-four.

Questions

Q1: What can happen when lightning strikes a building?

A: Lightning can cause buildings to catch on fire.

Q2: What other activities made Ben Franklin famous?

A: Franklin also helped write the U.S. Constitution and he invented bifocals.

Q3: What is one invention that is needed to keep people safe today and why?

A: Sometimes people are attacked by mountain lions while they are hiking. An invention to scare away mountain lions while hiking would keep people safe.

Ask participants to consider the challenges they may face with Question Generation in their class as you review Exhibit 5.35. Refer participants to Chapter Two for additional ideas to support Question Generation.

Participants can now go back to the lesson-plan template and the practice text to complete the possible questions section in Exhibit 5.36. As they are writing, encourage participants to share with one another the skills that are needed to generate questions and ideas for developing these skills.

EXHIBIT 5.34. Turn and Talk: Question Generation

- At your table, discuss the differences between teacher-generated questions and student-generated questions about text.

- What do students gain from asking their own questions?

EXHIBIT 5.35. Avoid the Pitfalls: Question Generation

Students struggle to write questions.

- Provide an answer from the text and have students make it into a question.

- Practice writing factual questions first that are taken directly from the text, starting with who, what, when, and where questions.

- Use question stems or fill-in-the-blank structures to scaffold writing a variety of question types.

Students write questions but the quality isn't high.

- Have students read a variety of questions and discuss which ones are high quality and why (e.g., well-written, ask important information, not vague, stay with the text).

- Increase accountability. It's more important to write a good question if someone is going to read it or use it.

  ○ Use questions as an exit ticket.

  ○ Play "pass a question." Have students trade questions with another group. See which groups can find all the answers.

  ○ Have each group work to create a class quiz or game by coming up with important and well-written questions.

  ○ Gather the best questions and use them in a warm-up for the next class.

EXHIBIT 5.36. Question Generation:
Lesson-Planning Activity

- Review _____. Write three questions and answers.
- Discuss with a partner:
  - What information or skills are needed to answer each question?
  - What are some ways to encourage students to write a variety of questions?

EXHIBIT 5.37. Teacher-Led Wrap Up: Content Focus

- Review key ideas and responses with the class.
- Revisit student predictions and check for accuracy.
- Have students write a longer summary of the text or use another writing activity.
- Create a concept map connecting concepts in this reading or connecting these concepts with other topics in your curriculum.
- Provide additional information about important vocabulary terms.

Review

The final CSR strategy is Review. In their learning logs, students write one or two sentences containing the most important information from the entire passage. Teachers encourage students to look back at the text and also to review their learning logs, especially the gists. Students then share their Review statements with their small group, providing evidence for why their Review contains the most important information. After students have shared briefly in their groups, the teacher brings the group back together for a final whole-group Wrap Up. Two goals of the whole-group Wrap Up are to review important content and to highlight one or more CSR strategies. Exhibits 5.37 and 5.38 provide ideas for focusing on the content or strategies during the whole-class Wrap Up.

Have participants work in pairs to complete their lesson plan template with the practice text. They can write the Review statement and share with a partner. Next, model for participants how one might lead the whole-class Review. For this model, the presenter is the teacher and the participants become the class. Provide a content focus (e.g., briefly reviewing predictions to see if they match what the passage was about) and

---

EXHIBIT 5.38. Teacher-Led Wrap Up: Strategy Focus

- Focus on one strategy and conduct a minilesson.
  - For example, highlight the gists from one section and reinforce information contained in high-quality gists.
  - For example, identify key clunks students had and discuss which fix-up strategies were used to solve the clunks.
- Have students review their learning logs before handing them in to be sure that all information is included and done well.
- Have students circle their best gist and question. Those will be the ones the teachers will grade.
- Have students debrief about the functioning of their group by identifying one thing they did well and one thing they need to work on next time. Share with the class.

---

a strategy focus (e.g., review one or two clunks and the fix-up strategies that could be used to figure them out). Discuss with the group ideas they have for leading the whole-class Review.

Putting It All Together: CSR in Cooperative Groups

As you read in Chapter Three, cooperative learning is used in CSR to support student-led discussions about text. Thus, a key part of professional development is having participants practice CSR, in its entirety, in cooperative groups. We have found that using a text that participants find difficult is effective because it allows participants to genuinely use the strategies as they grapple to understand text with a small group of their peers. This portion of PD takes forty-five minutes to one hour. Select a short but difficult text. Instruct participants to use CSR as themselves. They do not need to pretend to be school-age. Guide the group through CSR, just as a teacher would lead the class.

1. Divide participants into groups of four and assign roles. Give participants a few minutes to review their roles. In their groups, participants complete the same "Our CSR Roles" sheet (Form 3.2) that students will use when they learn CSR.

2. Hand out all materials (learning log; reading, divided into three sections; and cue cards).

3. Lead the whole-group Preview.

4. Provide time for participants to go through the during-reading strategies, Click and Clunk and Get the Gist, and the after-reading strategies, Question Generation and Review. Use a timer to monitor.

5. Bring the group together and conduct a whole-group Wrap Up, including a short content focus and strategy focus.

6. Debrief by asking participants what they like about CSR, what challenges they might anticipate when implementing it with their students, and whether they have any questions.

Closing

Before participants leave PD, it is helpful for them to have some time to plan how they will introduce CSR to their students and incorporate CSR into their instructional routines. Even twenty to thirty minutes to consider applications of CSR in their classroom can be integral to transferring what was learned in PD to classroom practice. Teachers should consider the content they teach and the needs of their students as they plan a timeline for introducing and using the strategies (see Exhibit 5.39).

The PD we have described here covers the basics of CSR and what we would generally cover in two days of PD. The amount of time can vary depending on how much time participants spend practicing the CSR strategies, how many questions they have, and how much time they devote to planning for CSR instruction in their classes. In the next chapter, we discuss other possible PD opportunities as well as ways to provide ongoing support to teachers.

EXHIBIT 5.39. Planning for CSR

When will I teach CSR?

- Consider content area, class schedule, and student needs

- How many days each week and for how long

What do I need to get started?

- CSR materials, textbook, and supplemental readings

What skills do I need to teach my students?

- How to work in cooperative groups

- Other skills as needed to use strategies

What CSR support is available?

- School or district structures to support CSR implementation

- Time to collaborate with colleagues to share resources, challenges, and successes

CHAPTER 6

Supporting CSR Through Coaching and Booster Sessions

> *I know that the booster meetings, for me, were huge, just motivation-wise, especially at points in the year. We did the winter one where you're just dragging and it's, you know, the middle of the year. New ideas, and being able to talk with other people who are doing it. It's been a really great experience; I'm glad I decided to do this.*
>
> —MIDDLE SCHOOL LANGUAGE ARTS TEACHER

> *I especially liked the last booster session that we had where everyone brought in an idea of one thing that was working with CSR. I liked that. I don't think teachers have enough built-in time to collaborate together. You know, the teachers supporting each other.*
>
> —READING INTERVENTION TEACHER

Simply attending a PD workshop rarely provides teachers with sufficient information and skill to put a new instructional approach into practice.[1] To implement CSR well, most teachers benefit from additional support. Over the years, we have honed the ways we assist teachers. In this chapter, we describe the booster sessions that we offer periodically as well as the in-class support we provide. Both of these options include tailoring support to the needs of specific teachers.

Booster Sessions

Booster sessions are short PD sessions (one to two hours) that can occur after school or during regularly scheduled school PD time (e.g., late-start days, during professional learning community time). The focus is on fine-tuning a specific skill or strategy and engages teachers in reflecting on implementation successes and challenges. For each session, teachers are asked to bring in materials or student artifacts. In the absence of a

PD provider or coach, teachers have successfully run these sessions on their own, using the booster session frameworks provided here as a guide or creating their own. Regardless of who facilitates the booster sessions, they are designed for teachers who have already learned CSR and are currently implementing it in their classrooms.

The topics for booster sessions should be decided on collaboratively by teachers and the PD team. Not all teachers' needs are the same. For example, for secondary teachers, successful implementation of CSR often hinges on the ability of teachers to align strategy instruction with their content-specific curriculum. Thus, many secondary teachers benefit from a booster session geared to selecting text to use for CSR. Teachers also vary in their experience with cooperative learning. For teachers new to cooperative learning, a booster session focused on cooperative-learning routines and structures is beneficial. Some teachers and their students benefit from a review of the CSR strategies.

Strategy Booster Sessions

Strategy booster sessions focus on the four CSR strategies: Preview, Click and Clunk, Get the Gist, and Wrap Up. Depending on teachers' needs and preferences, as well as the time available for PD, schools may elect to conduct one or more of these sessions.

Booster Session One: Focus on Preview

Goals (may vary depending on teacher needs):

- Reflect on Preview
- Fine-tune planning and delivery of Preview
  - *Focus:* Maximizing student participation
  - *Focus:* Selecting words and concepts to preteach

Preparation for teachers:

- [Teachers bring with them] Textbooks or other text sources that will be used for a CSR lesson
- Review PD materials on Preview

Materials:

- "Selecting Words and Concepts to Preteach" (Exhibit 6.1)
- "CSR Lesson-Planning Template" (Form 5.1)

During the booster:

- Begin with a reflection that focuses on Preview. Provide teachers with time to share one success and one challenge or question.
- Review key components of the Preview strategy, referring to CSR resources such as the teacher cue cards (see Appendix A).

- Highlight ways to maximize student participation during Preview:

  - *Five-finger background knowledge checks.* Ask students to hold up their hand with one to five fingers to indicate how familiar they are with a topic. This is a quick read that may help teachers make decisions about building background knowledge.

  - *Write-share.* For brainstorm and predict, students first write in their learning logs on their own and then share briefly with the group. Use a timer to keep the pace moving quickly and to encourage participation. Teachers can provide one minute to write and then one to two minutes to share in a small group.

  - *Whole-group share.* First, decide if whole-group sharing is needed. Sometimes if students are on track and sharing openly in their groups, a whole-group share is not necessary. Whole-group sharing can be used to model strong examples, to summarize key ideas, to emphasize metacognition, and to build background knowledge, especially about a new topic or unit of study. Options for sharing include having one or two students write their responses on the board while others share in groups, restating to the whole class what the teacher hears students share, asking students to share something they heard in their group, and asking one student to share and then another student to add to that idea or say why the information relates to the particular strategy or topic. In any case, whole-class sharing should not take very long.

- Review Exhibit 6.1, "Selecting Words and Concepts to Preteach." Use a student-level reading and model or work with a group to identify words and concepts to preteach. Discuss the selection process and ways to connect vocabulary to the topic of the reading.

EXHIBIT 6.1. Selecting Words and Concepts to Preteach

Introduction: A key step in the CSR process is for the teacher to preteach important vocabulary words or concepts that students will come across in the reading. Given the powerful relationship between vocabulary and comprehension, this step can be vital to helping students access and understand what they read. This practice also helps reinforce important concepts of the curricular unit or content area.

Note: Words that are pretaught are not the same as clunks that students identify on their own while reading. Pretaught words may be able to be figured out with fix-up strategies. They are selected because they are important based on the following guidelines and may require additional instruction. If a pretaught word lends itself to a fix-up strategy, point that out to students.

(Continued)

Ask yourself the following questions when selecting words and concepts to preteach:

- *Passage:* Which word(s) and concepts are important and useful to understanding the main idea of the passage?

- *Unit:* Which word(s) and concepts are important and useful to understanding the essential questions or big ideas of the unit?

- *Content area:* Which word(s) or concepts are important and useful to understanding key concepts in your discipline (e.g., social studies or science)?

- *Development of academic language:* Which word(s) or concepts support the development of academic language? Are there words that your students may not yet know in-depth (e.g., be familiar with but not fully understand)?

- *Support for ELLs:* Which words or concepts will be especially challenging for ELLs?

- Words with multiple meanings across contexts (e.g., *trigger, table, property, fault, cell, square, rut*):
  - *Social studies example:* The Constitution of the United States was built on the foundation that **powers** should be shared among the **branches** of government.
  - *Science example:* Calculate the **power** it takes for an **average** woman to climb a **flight** of stairs sixteen feet high.

- Process words that are essential to understanding the passage that carry across content areas (e.g., *contrast, illustrate, likewise, for instance*).
  - *Example:* The author **suggests** that alternative power sources, **although** initially more expensive, will decrease in costs as more power companies invest in their development.

- Idioms or words that imply cultural knowledge.
  - *Example:* Economists predict that the way to the **yellow brick road** for the US economy is a recommitment to investment in infrastructure.
  - *Example:* The Japanese stock market took a **nose dive** in response to the job forecast in the United States this week.

- As you implement CSR, it may be challenging to narrow down the number of words to preteach to only two or three. Form 6.1 can help guide you to select the most appropriate words to preteach. You may want to provide additional instruction and follow-up activities outside of your CSR lesson to support deep understanding of important words and concepts.

FORM 6.1. Words and Concepts to Preteach During CSR Checklist Guide[2]

What words or concepts are your students unlikely to be familiar with?

_____

_____

_____

Of these words and concepts, which are essential to the understanding of the reading?

_____

_____

_____

Of these words and concepts, which are important to understanding the main themes of the unit or your discipline?

_____

_____

_____

What words or concepts support development of academic language (can be applied across academic disciplines)?

_____

_____

_____

What words might be especially challenging for English language learners?

Multiple-meaning words

_____

_____

_____

Process words

_____

_____

_____

Idioms or words that imply cultural knowledge

_____

_____

_____

- Provide time for teachers to plan the preview of a CSR lesson.
- Ask one or two teachers to do a practice teach of the Preview they developed or conduct a more informal discussion of the planning process.

Booster Session Two: Focus on Click and Clunk

Goals (may vary depending on teacher needs):

- Reflect on Click and Clunk using students' learning logs
- Fine-tune implementation
  - *Focus:* "Know Your Role and Use It!" (Exhibit 6.2)
  - *Focus:* Support students to use fix-up strategies

Preparation for teachers:

- [Teachers bring with them] A class set of learning logs and the reading that went with them
- Review PD materials on Click and Clunk

Materials:

- Short adult-level passage containing likely clunks
- "CSR Scoring Rubric" (Form 4.2)

During the booster:

- Begin with a reflection that focuses on Click and Clunk. Allow teachers time to look through their students' learning logs and to identify successes and potential challenges with clunks. Provide the Click and Clunk portion of the CSR rubric to guide reflections.
- Provide time to share reflections and ideas.
- Distribute Exhibit 6.3. Allow time to discuss examples and brainstorm solutions.
- Explain the "Know Your Role and Use It!" tune-up minilesson (Exhibit 6.2) and, if there is time, practice with a short passage during the booster session. In this activity, teachers focus only on the Click and Clunk strategy and review the strategy in phases. First, the teacher reads a short section of text with the class with the teacher as the Clunk Expert. The passage should include plenty of clunks for students to identify that can be figured out with fix-up strategies. The teacher models the use of fix-up strategies as needed, guided by the Clunk Expert cue card. Then the teacher debriefs with the class the steps for Click and Clunk and how the fix-up strategies and resources were used. Next, the teacher asks students to read the subsequent text section in their groups and to apply the strategy. The Clunk Expert has his or her role card and also a table tent (index card folded in half) that says Clunk Expert. This way the teacher and students know who is leading the group. The teacher asks students to reflect on the process, sharing

EXHIBIT 6.2. Know Your Role and Use It!

Clunk Expert

Goals:

- To fine-tune the use of any one of the CSR expert roles

- To fine-tune the use of that same CSR strategy

We provide the Clunk Expert role as an example, but this lesson can also be used to fine-tune the Gist Expert role, the Question Expert role, and the Leader role. When using this lesson to focus on the Leader role, the class will engage in all other CSR strategies as well so that the Leaders can guide their groups through the strategies.

Procedure:

- Select a short passage for students to read.

- Set expectations for the target role.
  - Assign the Clunk Expert role to one student in each group. Clunk experts can wear an expert pin, name plate, or name badge. This allows students and the teacher to easily identify students in this role.
  - Tell students they will focus on just clunks today.
  - Review the strategy procedures and the Clunk Expert Cue Card with the class.

- Focus on just one strategy during reading.
  - *First section of text:* The teacher assumes the target role. Go through the first section as one large group, with the teacher reading the section aloud and performing the Clunk Expert role.
  - *Second and third sections:* Students apply the strategy in their groups. Focus on the strategy with your feedback to individual groups. Bring the class together between sections to give feedback and suggestions.

- Reflect on the lesson.
  - Hand out one "Clunk Group-Work Debrief" (Form 6.2) to each group.
  - Provide time for students to complete the debrief.
  - Debrief as a class and set goals for the next lesson.

- Repeat this lesson as needed with additional roles (see Forms 6.3, 6.4, and 6.5). You may also do a complete CSR lesson and provide time for students to complete the Group-Work Debrief as part of the Wrap Up.

FORM 6.2. Clunk Group-Work Debrief

Group Names: _____

_____

Date: _____

	YES (2)	SOMETIMES (1)	NOT REALLY (0)
We all have clunks and definitions in our learning logs.			
The **Clunk Expert** guided the group to share clunks and to use fix-up strategies to figure out the meaning of clunks.			
We put each definition back into the sentence with the clunk to be sure it made sense.			
We all participated in the discussion and helped each other.			
TOTAL SCORE			

One thing we did really well: _____

_____

_____

_____

One thing we could do better next time: _____

_____

_____

_____

FORM 6.3. Leader Group-Work Debrief

Group Names: _____

_____

Date: _____

	YES (2)	SOMETIMES (1)	NOT REALLY (0)
The **Leader** kept the group moving through all the parts of CSR.			
The **Leader** kept track of time.			
The **Leader** guided the group to write and share their review statements.			
We all participated in discussions and helped each other.			
TOTAL SCORE			

One thing we did really well: _____

_____

_____

_____

One thing we could do better next time: _____

_____

_____

_____

FORM 6.4. Gist Group-Work Debrief

Group Names: _____

_____

Date: _____

	YES (2)	SOMETIMES (1)	NOT REALLY (0)
The **Gist Expert** guided the group to come up with the most important who or what before writing gists.			
All students wrote their own gists before discussing.			
The **Gist Expert** guided the group to share and discuss the quality of gists.			
We worked together to select the best gist or to write a "super gist."			
TOTAL SCORE			

One thing we did really well: _____

_____

_____

_____

One thing we could do better next time: _____

_____

_____

_____

FORM 6.5. Question Expert Group-Work Debrief

Group Names: _____

_____

Date: _____

	YES (2)	SOMETIMES (1)	NOT REALLY (0)
The **Question Expert** guided the group to write different types of questions (Right There, Think and Search, Author and You).			
All students wrote their own questions and answers in their learning logs.			
The **Question Expert** guided the group to ask and answer their questions.			
We all participated and helped each other.			
TOTAL SCORE			

One thing we did really well: _____

_____

_____

_____

One thing we could do better next time: _____

_____

_____

_____

EXHIBIT 6.3. Fix-Up Strategies: Reflection

Read each transcript and discuss in your group:

- What is going well?
- Identify any problem(s).
- Identify possible next steps for instruction.

Example One

Student 1: How about the word *disembark*? *Embark* means to go someplace, and *dis* means not, so it means not go anywhere?

Student 2: So, if we used prefixes and suffixes, then what strategy would that be?

Student 3: I don't know.

Example Two

Student 3: I have *precedent*.

Student 4: Anyone know what that means?

Student 2: If no one knows what *precedent* is, I'll grab a dictionary.

Student 1: Well, you need to reread the sentence first.

[Group does not reread but continues to discuss.]

Student 2: So . . . pro-cedent. The prefix is *pro*.

Student 1: *Pre,* that's *pre*.

Student 2: *Pre* meaning before.

Student 1: Uh huh.

Student 2: So what else? *Pre* is before.

Student 1: Do you want to grab a dictionary?

Student 3: Yeah.

Example Three

Student 1: OK. *Widespread.* What do you think *widespread* means?

Student 2: Let's read the sentence: Driven by des-per-ation caused by widespread economic desperation . . .

Student 3: Depression.

Student 2: Depression. Right. Depression. So I think *widespread* means, it's like, it's like a large amount of something. The depression was everywhere.

Student 3: So it's spread wide. That's number three. Read number three.

Student 2: I'm reading it. Look for prefixes, suffixes, or roots. Break the word apart and look for smaller words you know.

Student 3: Oh, you did say wide and spread.

Student 1: We got it! A large amount of something. The depression was widespread. It was spread wide.

what worked and what did not. It is important for the teacher to confirm that students are identifying clunks on their own, using the fix-up strategies, discussing definitions, and putting definitions back into the text to check that they make sense. After debriefing and perhaps modeling again how to use one or more of the fix-up strategies, the teacher directs students to read another section. Students should be becoming more systematic in their application of the Click and Clunk strategy.

- Discuss with teachers their next steps for fine-tuning Click and Clunk. The "Know Your Role and Use It!" activity (Exhibit 6.2) can be used to tune up any of the strategies and is particularly useful when students are overlooking the critical steps and discussion features that go along with a strategy.

Booster Session Three: Focus on Get the Gist

Goals (may vary depending on teacher needs):

- Reflect on Get the Gist using students' learning logs
- Fine-tune implementation

  ○ *Focus:* Helping students write and discuss high-quality gists

Preparation for teachers:

- [Teachers bring with them] A class set of learning logs and the reading that went with them.
- Review PD materials on Get the Gist

Materials:

- "CSR Scoring Rubric" (Form 4.2)
- Exhibit 6.4, "Gist Tune-up Sample"

During the booster:

- Begin with a reflection that focuses on Get the Gist. Ask teachers how they evaluate the quality of student gists.
- Have teachers work in pairs or small groups to evaluate a class set of gists using the "CSR Scoring Rubric." Discuss questions or challenges that arise. Finding the

EXHIBIT 6.4. Gist Tune-Up Sample

Benjamin Franklin's Kite Experiment

Ben Franklin hypothesized, or proposed, that lightning was a stream of electricity created in the clouds during a storm. In 1752, he formulated an experiment to test his idea. He planned to use a kite and metal key to direct the flow of electricity from clouds to the ground. If he could show conduction of the electrical stream through these materials, then he could prove that lightning was made of electricity.

1. With your group, decide the most important who or what in this passage.

2. Now, write the most important ideas about the who or what.

3. On your own, write your gist.

Discuss your gist with your group:

___Do all gists contain the most important who or what and the most important information about the passage? If not, rewrite.

___Are all gists complete sentences that are about ten words or less? If not, rewrite.

Below, write a "super gist" that contains the important information from this section and is a complete sentence of about ten words or less. Be prepared to share your gist with the class.

---

main idea of a section and synthesizing it into a concise statement is difficult for many students. Taking time to evaluate the quality of students' work is particularly useful for this strategy. Have teachers determine what proportion of their classes are struggling and proficient.

- Review with teachers how to break down the gist-writing process for students who are struggling. Offer the idea of a gist tune-up activity that refocuses students on the components of Get the Gist as well as the types of discussions that support high-quality gist writing. Exhibit 6.4 shows a sample of a gist practice activity. Additional gist practice activities can be found in Chapter Four. After students complete the warm-ups, the teacher can then continue to model evaluating gists by writing the super gists from each group on the board. The class can compare gists and discuss their important features.

- Discuss with teachers their next steps for fine-tuning Get the Gist.

Booster Session Four: Wrap Up

Goals (may vary depending on teacher needs):

- Reflect on Wrap Up
- Fine-tune implementation
- *Focus:* Get the most from the teacher Wrap Up

Preparation for teachers:

- Review PD materials on Wrap Up
- [Teachers bring with them] A class set of learning logs and the reading that went with them

During the booster:

- Begin with a reflection that focuses on Generating Questions and Review. Encourage teachers to share their successes and challenges.
- Review the steps to Wrap Up and the PD materials related to conducting a whole-class Wrap Up. The PD materials offer several ideas. Teachers may work on one of the ideas provided or create their own activities. Divide teachers into two groups. One group focuses on content-focused whole-class Wrap Up activities and the other group focuses on strategy-focused whole-class Wrap Up activities. Provide time for teachers to develop activities based on student needs (identified from learning logs) and content goals (identified from text and units).
- Have teachers share their activities along with a rationale for why they selected them.

Additional Booster Session Topics

Following is a list of possible topics and agenda items for additional booster sessions. Because these topics will vary depending on instructional needs, they are offered in a menu format that leaves room for site-specific development. In many cases, schools or school districts already provide PD in these areas. For instance, a school district might focus on a specific method of classroom management or endorse a particular PD program for ELLs. In these cases, we recommend offering PD that integrates district methods with CSR.

- Fine-tuning cooperative learning
    - Teaching team building
    - Deepening discussions
    - Providing effective feedback during group work
- Text selection
    - Identifying high-quality readings
    - Aligning with the curriculum

- ○ Understanding the influence of text difficulty and length

- ○ Differentiating texts for diverse learners

- Supporting vocabulary learning with CSR

- ○ Integrating CSR with vocabulary instruction

- ○ Creating follow-up vocabulary activities

- ○ Addressing vocabulary needs of ELLs

- Supporting ELLs

- ○ Connecting CSR with high-quality instruction for ELLs

- ○ Developing academic language through CSR

- ○ Supporting ELLs during cooperative group work

- Integrating technology use into CSR lessons

- ○ May include specific strategies to integrate technology effectively such as interactive whiteboards (e.g., Smartboard, Promethean), laptop computers, or iPads into CSR instruction.

- CSR celebrations

- ○ Every spring we have a "celebrations" booster session at which teachers are asked to share a CSR success. They may bring an activity, student artifacts, or a personal story. Teachers love the celebrations booster. It is a way to highlight accomplishments and to share ideas.

In-Class Support

Teachers who participate in CSR PD bring with them unique needs and preferences. Beliefs, attitudes, knowledge, and context influence how teachers take up new strategies they have learned in PD and whether or not they continue to use them. Coaches must work to understand and meet each teacher's specific needs and to provide helpful feedback that is applicable to their current teaching situations. In-class support structures vary by school district. As with the booster sessions described previously, implementation and sustainability are often dependent on the extent to which the new strategies align with existing practices. Coaching is no different. Many of the school districts in which we have worked support a cognitive coaching model,[3] but other models of coaching and support can be used as well.

Whenever possible, we recommend taking time to visit teachers in classrooms. In-class coaching activities should be supportive and nonevaluative. Depending on a teacher's preference, in-class support can involve observation with feedback, modeling parts of CSR, or co-teaching. We have asked a few of the teachers we have worked with to share their thoughts about the in-class support they have received from coaches. Here are some of their comments:

Lisa McKinney: If I tried something on Monday or Tuesday and it wasn't working well, then I could say, "[Coach], if you are coming in on Thursday, would you mind modeling this because I don't think the way I am doing it is effective enough." It was very beneficial!

Mark Farah: Well, the feedback, having another adult in the room who really knows what should go on, and what is going on, just another set of eyes, and ears and hands. And that was cool. I felt very free then, to spend time with groups of kids like she was doing. She tended to stay more . . . longer with groups, which is fine, and then I was able to keep the other ones going, and interact with them. It was good. I think teaching is a really lonely profession and having other adults, especially experienced adults, in is helpful. And I have never been shy about that and I always enjoyed it.

Maria Catalan: My coach was out here a lot, and she always had good ideas at the end of the day and it was nice to try them the next time we did CSR. I know she also did a lesson or two for me, and my kids just absolutely loved it. They loved her; they were always asking when she was going to come back. So, it was nice to, you know, to almost co-teach, or you know, have somebody else do an activity and support the kids instead of vice versa.

In addition, planning meetings and follow-up feedback—debriefing sessions are essential. Suggestions should be specific and teachers should be central to planning. Coaches or teacher observers may use the "CSR Observation Guide: Strategy Checklist" (Form 6.6), "CSR Observation" (Form 6.7), and "CSR Action Plan" (Form 6.8) to guide planning meetings, classroom visits, and follow-up debriefing sessions. Mr. Farah commented, "The feedback was very helpful. We would have a conversation if we had time, either one of us, and then I would get an e-mail from my coach, and she focused me very well, and talked about the things that I did well and then, here is the way that I could grow! And I appreciated that. And, she was right on. She knew what we were to do."

FORM 6.6. CSR Observation Guide: Strategy Checklist

Use a strategy checklist during coaching or other CSR observations.

PREVIEW	
Checklist	**Notes**
☐ Teacher states the topic.	
☐ Teacher presents important vocabulary and concepts using pictures, charts, graphic organizers, short videos, and brief descriptions (two to three).	
☐ Students preview the text (read headings, subheadings, bold words, charts, etc.).	
☐ Students brainstorm and write what they already know about the topic in their learning logs. Students share briefly with their partner or group. Teacher builds background knowledge using pictures, charts, graphic organizers, short videos, and brief descriptions.	
☐ Students write predictions. Students share briefly with their partner or group. Teacher provides feedback.	
☐ Teacher states the purpose for reading.	

CLICK AND CLUNK	
Checklist	**Notes**
IDENTIFYING CLUNKS	
☐ Students identify words and ideas they don't understand.	
☐ Students write clunks in their learning log.	
☐ Students share clunks with their group.	
USE FIX-UP STRATEGIES	
☐ Students know the four fix-up strategies.	
☐ Students use fix-up strategies to figure out the meanings of clunks.	
☐ Students work together within their group to find meanings of clunks.	

GET THE GIST	
Checklist	**Notes**
☐ Students identify the most important who or what in the section and the most important information about the who or what.	
☐ Students write their own gist in their learning log.	
☐ Students share gists and provide feedback in group.	

FORM 6.6. (continued)

WRAP UP	
Checklist	**Notes**
QUESTIONS and ANSWERS ☐ Students write leveled questions (Right There, Think and Search, Author and You) and answers in their learning log. ☐ Students share questions with their group. REVIEW ☐ Students write one or two of the most important ideas from the entire passage in their learning log. ☐ Teacher guides students to share with their group and discuss why the ideas they have written are important. ☐ Teacher leads whole-group Wrap Up that reviews important content and highlights a specific CSR strategy.	

COOPERATIVE LEARNING	
Checklist	**Notes**
☐ Routines are used to manage materials and conduct group work. ☐ Students use CSR roles. ☐ All students participate in cooperative groups. ☐ Students help each other. ☐ Students share and discuss the quality of responses in their small groups for each strategy.	

FORM 6.7. CSR Observation

Teacher _____ Observer Date _____

Start Time _____ End Time _____

Preobservation notes:

Observation focus, if applicable:

Components of CSR

Reading materials used: _____

_____

_____

Before Reading

■	Teacher Preview	
■	Student Preview	

During Reading

■	Click and Clunk	
■	Gist	

After Reading

■	Question Generation	
■	Review	

Cooperative Grouping

■	Student engagement in roles	
■	Monitoring student work	

Post-observation notes and next steps:

FORM 6.8. CSR Action Plan

Teacher:	Coach:	Date:

List two or three instructional activities that are going well.

Check all that apply:

___Preview   ___Click and Clunk   ___Gist   ___Review

___Cooperative Learning   ___Text Selection   ___Differentiation   ___Other

CSR Challenge	Action Plan (next steps by teacher or coach)	Completed by or Person Responsible
1.		
2.		
3.		
4.		

To Sum Up

Reading comprehension strategies and cooperative learning are often considered higher-level practices that can be difficult for teachers to implement and sustain. Yet, the teachers we have worked with over the years tell us that CSR can be easily integrated into existing classroom instruction to help students in heterogeneous classes think more deeply about what they are learning as they read grade-level (or higher) text. The key to successful implementation for most teachers is in-depth, context-specific PD opportunities that include follow-up booster sessions and in-class support.

Part IV

Appendixes

Classroom-Ready CSR Materials

The following items are included in Appendix A:

- Learning Log for Informational Text
- Learning Log for Narrative Text
- Student Cue Cards
- Teacher Cue Cards
- Roots
- Prefixes
- Suffixes
- Cognate List
- Question Stems

Learning Log for Informational Text

Name _____ **Date** _____

Today's Topic _____

Before Reading: Preview

Brainstorm: Connections to prior knowledge

_____

_____

_____

_____

_____

_____

Predict: What I might learn about the topic

_____

_____

_____

_____

_____

_____

During Reading: Section One

CLUNKS		**DEFINITIONS**	
_____	=	_____	1 2 3 4
_____	=	_____	1 2 3 4
_____	=	_____	1 2 3 4

Gist:

_____

During Reading: Section Two

CLUNKS		**DEFINITIONS**	
_____	=	_____	1 2 3 4
_____	=	_____	1 2 3 4
_____	=	_____	1 2 3 4

Gist:

_____

Learning Log for Informational Text (continued)

During Reading: Section Three

CLUNKS   DEFINITIONS

_____ = _____ 1 2 3 4

_____ = _____ 1 2 3 4

_____ = _____ 1 2 3 4

Gist:

_____

After Reading: Wrap Up

Questions: Write questions and answers.

_____

_____

_____

_____

_____

_____

_____

_____

_____

_____

_____

Review: Write one or two of the most important ideas in this passage. Be prepared to justify your ideas.

_____

_____

_____

_____

_____

_____

_____

_____

_____

_____

Learning Log for Narrative Text

Name _____ **Date** _____

Today's Topic _____

Before Reading: Preview

Brainstorm: Connections to prior knowledge. What happened in the passage last time we read?

_____

_____

_____

_____

_____

_____

Predict: What might happen today?

_____

_____

_____

_____

_____

_____

During Reading: Section One

CLUNKS		DEFINITIONS	
_____	=	_____	1 2 3 4
_____	=	_____	1 2 3 4
_____	=	_____	1 2 3 4

Gist:

_____

During Reading: Section Two

CLUNKS		DEFINITIONS	
_____	=	_____	1 2 3 4
_____	=	_____	1 2 3 4
_____	=	_____	1 2 3 4

Gist:

_____

Learning Log for Narrative Text (continued)

During Reading: Section Three

CLUNKS **DEFINITIONS**

_____ = _____ 1 2 3 4

_____ = _____ 1 2 3 4

_____ = _____ 1 2 3 4

Gist:

_____

After Reading: Wrap Up

Questions: Write questions and answers.

_____

_____

_____

_____

_____

_____

_____

_____

_____

Review: Write one or two of the most important ideas in this passage. Be prepared to justify your ideas.

_____

_____

_____

_____

_____

_____

_____

_____

_____

CSR Leader

Job Description

The Leader's job is to guide the group through all the steps of CSR. The Leader keeps track of time, keeps the group working, and makes sure everyone works together.

DURING READING

Read

- Who would like to read the next section?

Click and Clunk

- Write your clunks in your learning log.
- Clunk Expert, please help us.

Get the Gist

- It's time to Get the Gist. Gist Expert, help us.

[Repeat all of the steps in this section.]

AFTER READING

Wrap Up

- It's time to ask questions. Question Expert, please help us.

Compliments and Suggestions

[Lead the group to review what worked and what can be changed for next time.]

- Something that went well today was _____.

- Next time we need to work on _____.
- Is there anything else that would help us do better next time?

Fix-Up
Strategies

DURING READING

- Reread the sentence with the clunk and look for key ideas to help you figure out the word. Think about what makes sense.

- Reread the sentences before and after the sentence with the clunk, looking for clues that help you figure out the clunk.

- Break the word apart and look for word parts (prefixes, suffixes, root words) or smaller words you know.

- Look for a cognate that makes sense.

Clunk Expert

Job Description

The Clunk Expert makes sure that students write their clunks in their learning logs. The Clunk Expert also helps students use fix-up strategies to figure out the meaning of unknown words or ideas.

DURING READING

Click and Clunk
- Who has a clunk?
- Does anyone know the meaning of the clunk?

If yes
- Please explain what the clunk means and why you think so.
- Let's reread the sentence and make sure that definition makes sense.

   [Check for understanding.]

If no, use fix-up strategies.

   [After you come up with a definition:]
- Write the definition in your learning log.
- Let's reread the sentence and make sure that definition makes sense.

CSR STUDENT CUE CARD

Get the Gist

DURING READING

- Find the most important who or what.
- Write the gist in your learning log.
  - Only the most important information
  - Leave out details
  - About ten words
  - Make a complete sentence
- Select the best gist or rewrite a "super gist."

CSR STUDENT CUE CARD

Gist Expert

Job Description

The Gist Expert makes sure that all students in the group write their own gists. The Gist Expert also leads the group in sharing gists and discussing the quality of the gists. High-quality gists contain the topic (the most important who or what) and the most important information about the topic. Gists should be about ten words.

DURING READING

Get the Gist

- What is the most important who or what in this section?

  [Ask students to share.]

- Everyone, think of your own gist and write it in your learning log.

  [When everyone is done:]

- Who would like to share their gist?

[Help your group come up with a gist that includes the most important information, leaves out the details, and contains about ten words.]

CSR STUDENT CUE CARD
Question Expert

Job Description

The Question Expert guides the group in coming up with questions that address important information from the reading. The Question Expert makes sure that students ask different levels of questions. The Question Expert checks to see that all students write questions and answers.

AFTER READING

Wrap Up

Let's think of some questions to check whether we really understood what we read. Write your questions and the answers in your learning log.

Remember to write different types of questions:

- Right There
- Think and Search
- Author and You

[After everyone is finished writing questions, ask:]

- Who would like to share his or her best question?

[Check that the question begins with who, what, when, where, why, or how.]

- Who would like to answer that question?
- Where did you find the information to answer that question?

CSR STUDENT CUE CARD
Question Types

LEVEL ONE: RIGHT THERE

- Questions can be answered in one sentence.
- Answers can be found word-for-word in the story.

Example: The answer to "What is the capital of Texas?" is found in one of the sentences of the text, "The capital of Texas is Austin."

LEVEL TWO: THINK AND SEARCH

- Questions can be answered by looking in the text.
- Answers require one sentence or more.
- Information is found in more than one place and put together.

Example: To answer "How did ranchers get their cattle to the markets?" several sentences are needed to describe the steps that are presented on different pages of the text.

LEVEL THREE: AUTHOR AND YOU

- Questions cannot be answered by using the text alone.
- Answers require thinking about what the reader just read, what the reader already knows, and how it fits together.

Example: To Answer, "How is the vampire bat different from other bats we have read about?" use information from the text and combine it with what you already have learned about other types of bats.

CSR TEACHER CUE CARD

Preview

Job Description
The teacher takes on the Leader role during Preview.

BEFORE READING

Strategy Description
- State the topic for today's reading.
  - Present a few important proper nouns, key vocabulary concepts, and brief definitions.
  - Use pictures, diagrams, video clips, and other cues to build background knowledge and help students make connections.
- Guide students to preview the text.
  - Read headings, subheadings, bold words, charts, and so on.
- Guide students to brainstorm what they already know about the topic.
  - Students write in their learning logs what they already know about the topic.
  - Students share briefly with a partner or with their group.
  - Call on students to share with the class.
- Provide additional support to build background knowledge and help students make connections (if needed).
- Guide students to make predictions.
  - Students write predictions in their learning logs.
  - Students share briefly with a partner or with their group.
  - Call on students to share with the class.
- State the purpose for reading.
  - Summarize student predictions to set a purpose for reading. For example, "As you read, consider the ways in which space travel may become more accessible to regular people like us."
  - Set a strategy focus, as needed. For example, "Today you will focus on writing high-quality gists that leave out important details."

Monitoring
- Check whether students make connections to what they already know about the topic.
- Check whether students preview the entire passage.
- Check whether students make predictions that are plausible, based on information from the Preview and any background knowledge building and vocabulary support you provided.

Feedback
- Help students distinguish between brainstorming and predicting.
- Help students make connections between the topic and their background knowledge.
- Build additional background knowledge.
- Connect what students are reading to their curriculum and real-life experiences.
- Summarize Preview statements and use them to set a purpose for reading.

CSR TEACHER CUE CARD

Click and Clunk

Job Description

The Clunk Expert guides students during Click and Clunk. The teacher's role is to monitor understanding, provide feedback, and provide additional instruction as needed.

DURING READING

Strategy Description

- Students read a short section of text.
- Students identify unknown words or ideas.
- Students work together in their groups to use the fix-up strategies to find the meaning of their clunks.

Fix-Up Strategies

- Reread the sentence with the clunk and look for key ideas to help you figure out the word.
- Reread the sentences before and after the clunk, looking for clues.
- Break the word apart and look for word parts (prefixes, suffixes, root words) or smaller words you know.
- Look for a cognate that makes sense.

Monitoring

- Check whether students identify clunks.
- Check whether students write their clunks in their learning logs.
- Check whether students use the fix-up strategies; suggest which fix-up strategy to use if needed.
- Check whether students can say how they figured out their clunks.
- Spotlight a group or individual who does an outstanding job and have them repeat what they said for the whole class.

Feedback

- Comment on appropriate clunk identification.
- Note when students use strategies appropriately (e.g., using prefixes, breaking down words, thinking about clues).
- Encourage students to try different fix-up strategies. Suggest which strategies to use as needed.
- Note explanations of clunks that make sense in the sentence and in context.
- Encourage students to say which fix-up strategies they used and how the strategies helped to figure out the word.

Additional Practice Ideas

- Model how to use one or more fix-up strategies to provide additional support.
- Have groups present clunks to the class and explain which fix-up strategy they thought was most helpful and why.
- Conduct minilessons on specific fix-up strategies.

Get the Gist

Job Description

The Gist Expert guides group members during Get the Gist. The teacher's role is to monitor understanding, provide feedback, and provide additional instruction as needed.

DURING READING

Strategy Description

- Students find the most important who or what.
- Students write the gist in about ten words (or fewer) in their learning logs.
- Students share their gists in their small groups.
- Students work together to select their best gist or come up with one "super gist."

Monitoring

- Check whether students identify the most important who or what.
- Check whether students identify the most important information about the who or what.
- Check whether students write their gist statements in about ten words (or fewer).
- Check whether gist statements are complete sentences.
- If students are working in groups, check whether students write individual gists before sharing with the group.
- Spotlight a group or individual who does an outstanding job and have them repeat what they said for the whole class.

Feedback

- Explain how to use clues to identify the most important who or what.
- Note when students exclude details from their gist statements.
- Comment on using only the most important information in gist statements.
- Encourage students to come to a consensus on gist statements through friendly debate with their partners or groups.

Additional Practice Ideas

- Model the strategy to provide additional support.
- Provide students with a list of statements about a central idea and ask students to combine the statements into a gist.
- After reading a short paragraph, have students write gists. Then post several student gists and evaluate them with the class. Students might vote for the gist they think is best.
- Have student groups select the best gist from several in a multiple-choice format and justify their choice.
- Have groups work together to identify the most important who or what and then use it to write individual gists.
- Provide an example gist with a common student mistake, such as including details. Ask students to correct the gist so that it contains only the most important information.

Question Generation

Job Description

The Question Expert guides students to write questions and answers about what they just read, using leveled question types. The teacher's role is to monitor understanding, provide feedback, and provide additional instruction as needed.

AFTER READING

Strategy Description

- Students write one or two sentences in their learning logs containing the most important information from the entire passage.
- Students share briefly with a partner or their group.
- Students share with the class.
- The teacher leads a final Wrap Up that reviews important content and highlights a specific CSR strategy.
- The teacher may add extension activities as needed.

Monitoring

- Check whether students write important information from the passage and not "fun facts."
- Check whether students write complete sentences.
- Check whether students share with their group and discuss why the ideas they have written are important. Friendly debate is expected.

Feedback

- Have students review gists to help students remember the most important ideas.
- Have students highlight important information.
- Model writing review statements.
- List important ideas and write a class Review statement with students.
- Discuss the difference between details that are not important to the overall passage and information that is important from a reading.

Roots[1]

ROOT	MEANING	EXAMPLES
anni, annu, enni	year	anniversary, annual, biennial, triennial, centennial, perennial
aqua, aque	water	aquatic, aquarium, aqueduct
aster, astro	star	astronaut, astronomy, asteroid
audi	sound	auditorium, audiotape, audition
biblio	book	bibliography
bio	life	biography, autobiography, biology, antibiotic
carn	meat	carnivorous, reincarnation
ced, cede	go, surrender, yield	proceed, precede, recede, concede
chrom	color	chromatology, monochrome, polychrome
chron	time	chronological, chronic, synchronize
corp	body	corpse, corporation
crac, crat	rule, ruler	autocrat, democracy
cruc	cross	crucifix, crucial
dem, demo	people	demography, democracy, epidemic
derm	skin	dermatology, epidermis, hypodermic
dict	speak, say	dictate, dictator, predict, dictionary
duc, duct	lead, make	produce, production, deduct
duo (du)	two	duo, duet, duplicate, duplex
emia, aemia	blood	anemia or anaemia (without enough red blood cells)
equ	equal	equal, equation, equator, equilateral
fac	make, do	manufacture, fact (something that is done), benefactor
geo	earth, soil, ground	geology, geography, geothermal
graph	writing, printing	graph, autograph, biography, geography, telegraph, photograph
hydro, hydr	water	hydrate, dehydrate, hydroplane
ject	throw	inject, eject, reject, projection
jur, jus	law	jury, justice
lect, leg	read, choose	legible, lecture, election
logue	speaking, writing	monologue, dialogue
magn, magni	great, big, large	magnify, magnificent
man(u)	hand	manufacture, manuscript, manicure
mand, mend	order, instruct, be in charge	demand, recommend
mar, mer	sea, pool	marine, mariner, marsh, mermaid
mater	mother	maternal, maternity, matriarch

ROOT	MEANING	EXAMPLES
meter, metri, metry	measure	meter, geometric, thermometer, diameter, perimeter
min	small	minority, minibike, minute, minimum
miss, mit, mitt	send	transmit, dismiss, submission, mission
mob, mot, mov	move	mobile, automobile, promote, motion, motionless, move, movie
mono	one	monarch, monologue, monorail, monoplane
morph	form, structure	metamorphosis, morphology
mor, mort	death	mortal, mortician, immortal
mut	change	mutant, mutability, mutate
neuro	nerve	neurology, neurosis, neurobiology
pater, patri	father	paternal, paternity, patriarch, patriotic
path, pathy	feeling, suffering	sympathy, apathy, empathy, telepathy
ped, pod	foot	pedal, pedometer, centipede, pedestrian, podiatrist, tripod
pel, puls	push	expel, pulse, pulsate, compel, propel
pend	hang, weigh	pendulum, pendant, suspend, pending
phon, phono	sound, voice	telephone, microphone, symphony
photo	light	photograph, photon
pneum, pneuma, pneumon	breath, lung	pneumatic, pneumonia
port	carry	portable, transport, import, export
psych	soul, spirit, mind	psychology, psychic
pyro, pyre	fire	pyrotechnics, pyromaniac, pyretic (causing fever)
punct	point, dot	punctual, punctuate, puncture
rupt	break	interrupt, disrupt, erupt, rupture
sci	know	science, conscious, unconscious
scrib, script	write	scribe, scribble, script, manuscript, inscription
sec, sect, seg	cut, part	dissect, section, segment
sign, signi	sign, mark, seal	sign, signal, signature, design
simil, simul	same, like, resembling	similar, simultaneous, facsimile (fax)
son	sound	sonar, resonate
sphere	ball, sphere	sphere, hemisphere, atmosphere
spir	breathe	inspire, respiration, perspiration
stroy, stru, struct	build or make	construct, destroy, instruct, structure, obstruct, instrument
tele	from far away, far off	telephone, telecast, television, teleport
temp, temp, tempor	time	tempo, temporary, contemporary

ROOT	MEANING	EXAMPLES
terr, ter	earth	territory, terrain, terrestrial
therm	heat	thermal, hypothermia, thermos, thermometer
tract, trah	draw, pull	tractor, traction, attract, subtract
vac	empty	vacuum, vacant, evacuate
vers, vert	turn	reverse, irreversible, convert
vid, vis	see	vision, visible, invisible, video, evident, revise, supervise
vit, via, viv, vivi	alive, life	vitamin, survive, revive

Prefixes[2]

PREFIX	MEANING	WORDS THAT CONTAIN THE PREFIX
a-	in, on, in the process of	asleep, ashore, aboard, awake, arise
a-, an-	not, without	atypical, anemia (without enough red blood cells)
ab-, abs-	apart, away from	abnormal, absent
anti-	against, the opposite	Antarctic, antifreeze, antiwar, antisocial, antibiotic
aqua-, aque-	water	aquarium, aqueous, aqueduct
auto-	self	autograph, autobiography, automobile, autopilot
bene	good	benefactor, benefit
bi- (bin, bis)	two, twice	binoculars, bisect, biennial
bio-	life, living	biology, biography, biohazard
centi-	one hundredth	centimeter, centipede
circu-, circum-	around	circumference, circumnavigate, circulatory
col-, com-, con-	with, together	collect, combine, communal, community, connect, conversation, congregate
contra-, counter-	against, opposite	contradict, contrast, counteract
de-	down, opposite of	defrost, depart, dehydrate, destruct
dec-	ten	decade
demi	half, part of	demigod
dia-, di-	through, across, between	diagonal, diameter, dialogue
dis-	not, negative	disrespect, discomfort, disadvantage
dyna-	power	dynamic (forceful, powerful), dynamite
e-, ex-	out of, away, from	exit, exhale, exclude, explosion, elect (choose out of)
em-, en-	cause to	empower, enable, enrage
equi-	equal	equidistant, equilateral, equivalent
ex- (see e-)		
exter-, extra-	outside of, beyond	external, exterior, extracurricular, extraordinary, extraterrestrial
fore-	before	forefather, forecast, foresee
frater	brother	fraternity, fraternize
hemi-	half	hemisphere
hyper-	over, above, more than normal	hyperactive, hypersensitive
hypo-	less than, below, under	hypothermia, hypothesis, hypodermic
il(l)-, im-, in-, ir-	not, without	illegal, impossible, inappropriate, incredible, irregular

PREFIX	MEANING	WORDS THAT CONTAIN THE PREFIX
il(l)-, im-, in-	in, into, towards, inside	imbibe (drink in, take in), invade, inland
inter-, intro-	among, within, between	international, introduce, interact, interpret
intra-	within	intrastate, intramural, intravenous
ir- (see il-)		
macro-	large	macroscopic, macrocosm, macroeconomics
mal-	bad	malfunction, malformed, malnutrition
mater-	mother	maternal, maternity, matricide
micro-	small	microscope, microwave, microorganism
mid-	middle	midyear, midnight, midway
milli	thousand	millimeter, millisecond
mis-	bad, wrongly, not	misunderstand, misbelieve, misjudge, misinform
mono-	one, single	monologue, monarchy, monoplane
multi-	many	multipurpose, multimillionaire, multimedia
non-	not	nonfiction, nonviolence, nonsense
octa-	eight	octagon
out-	more than	outrun, outsmart, outstanding
over-	too much, completely, outer	overtime, overcharge, overjoyed, overcoat
pater-	father	paternal, paternity, patricide
per-	for each, through	perennial (through the years, year after year)
peri-	around	perimeter, periscope (a scope that sees around corners)
poly-	many, several	polygon, polymorph
post-	after (in time or order)	postgraduate, postpone, postdate
pre-	before	prepay, prefix, predict (tell before)
pro- (por-, pur-)	for, forward	pronoun, prologue (words that come before the main story)
re-	back, again	return, repaint, restate, recalculate, renew
semi-	half, partly, lower	semicircle, semicolon, semiconscious
sub-	under, below, almost	submarine, submerge, subsoil, subsurface
super-, sur-	over, above	superstar, supernatural, superhuman, surpass
sur- (see super-)		
syn-, sym-, syl-, sys-	with, together, acting together	symphony, synchronize, symmetry
tele-	distant, far off	telescope, telephone, television, telegraph
to-	this	today, tonight, tomorrow

PREFIX	MEANING	WORDS THAT CONTAIN THE PREFIX
tra-, trans-, tres-	across	transatlantic, transport (carry across), traverse (go from one place to another), trespass
tri-	three	triangle, tricycle, tripod
ultra-	beyond, extreme	ultraviolet, ultrasonic, ultramicroscope
un-	not	uncooked, unacceptable, untrue
un-	undo something (an action)	unplug, untie, undo, unfold
uni-	one, together	universe, uniform, unison, unicorn, unicycle
under-	beneath, below, not enough	underarm, undercharge, underground, underdeveloped
with-	back, against	withdraw, withhold, withstand

Suffixes[3]

SUFFIX	MEANING	EXAMPLES
-s, -es	more than one, plural form of a noun	cats, boxes
-ed	past tense of a verb	sailed
-ing	progressive tense of a verb	jumping, racing
-ly	like, to extent of, turns a noun into an adverb	slowly, lovely
-er, -or (agent)	turns a verb into a noun (agent)	runner, professor
-tion, -ation, ition	being, the result of (noun)	action, transition, vacation
-able, -ible	capable of being	loveable, incredible
-al, -ial	like, suitable for, pertaining to	global, logical, partial
-y	quality, somewhat like, turns a noun into an adjective	funny
-ness	act of, condition of	kindness
-ity, -ty	condition of, quality of	activity
-ment	to form	merriment
-ic	like, having the nature of, turns a noun into an adverb	historic
-ous, -eous, -ious	characterized by, having quality of, turns a noun into an adjective	hideous, spacious
-en	made of, make	quicken, thicken
-er (comparative)	more than (comparative)	bigger
-ive, -ative, -tive	of, belonging to, quality of, turns a word into an adjective	alternative, pensive
-ful	full of	wonderful
-less	without	effortless
-est	superlative (comparative)	strongest

Cognate List[4]

ENGLISH	SPANISH
A	
accident	*accidente*
accidental	*accidental*
accompany (to)	*acompañar*
acrobatic	*acrobático(a)*
active	*activo(a)*
activities	*actividades*
admire (to)	*admirar*
admit (to)	*admitir*
adopt (to)	*adoptar*
adoption	*adopción*
adult	*adulto*
adventure	*aventura*
African	*africano*
agent	*agente*
air	*Aire*
alarm	*alarma*
allergic	*alérgico*
anaconda	*anaconda*
animal	*animal*
announce (to)	*anunciar*
appear (to)	*aparecer*
appetite	*apetito*
area	*área*
arithmetic	*aritmética*
artist	*artista*
association	*asociación*
astronomer	*astrónomo*
atmosphere	*atmósfera*
attention	*atención*
August	*agosto*
autograph	*autógrafo*
automobile	*automóvil*
B	
baby	*bebé*
banana	*banana*
banjo	*banjo*

ENGLISH	SPANISH
bicycle	*bicicleta*
biography	*biografía*
blouse	*blusa*
boat	*bote*
brilliant	*brillante*
C	
cabin	*cabina*
cable	*cable*
cafeteria	*cafetería*
calendar	*calendario*
camera	*cámara*
camouflage	*camuflaje*
canyon	*cañón*
captain	*capitán*
capture (to)	*capturar*
carpenter	*carpintero*
castle	*castillo*
catastrophe	*catástrofe*
cause	*causa*
celebrate (to)	*celebrar*
celebration	*celebración*
cement	*cemento*
center	*centro*
centimeter	*centímetro*
ceramic	*cerámica*
cereal	*cereal*
ceremony	*ceremonia*
chimney	*chimenea*
chimpanzee	*chimpancé*
cholera	*cólera*
circle	*círculo*
circular	*circular*
circus	*circo*
class	*clase*
coast	*costa*
collection	*colección*
colony	*colonia*

ENGLISH	SPANISH	ENGLISH	SPANISH
color	color	dictator	dictador
committee	comité	different	diferente
common	común	difficult	difícil
company	compañía	dinosaur	dinosaurio
complete	completo(a)	direction	dirección
completely	completamente	directions	direcciones
computer	computadora	directly	directamente
concert	concierto	director	director
confetti	confeti	disappear (to)	desaparecer
confusing	confuso	disaster	desastre
confusion	confusión	discrimination	discriminación
constellation	constelación	discuss (to)	discutir
construction	construcción	disgrace	desgracia
contagious	contagioso(a)	distance	distancia
continent	continente	distribute (to)	distribuir
continue (to)	continuar	doctor	doctor
contract	contrato	dollar	dólar
contribution	contribución	double	doble
cost	costo, coste	dragon	dragón
coyote	coyote	dynamite	dinamita
crocodile	cocodrilo	**E**	
cross	cruz	electric	eléctrico(a)
culture	cultura	elephant	elefante
curious	curioso(a)	enormous	enorme
D		energy	energía
December	diciembre	English	inglés
decide (to)	decidir	enter (to)	entrar
decoration	decoración	escape (to)	escapar
delicate	delicado(a)	especially	especialmente
dentist	dentista	examine (to)	examinar
depend (to)	depender	exclaim	exclamar
deport (to)	deportar	explosion	explosión
describe (to)	describir	exotic	exótico(a)
desert	desierto	extra	extra
destroy (to)	destruir	extraordinary	extraordinario(a)
detain (to)	detener	**F**	
determine (to)	determinar	family	familia
diamond	diamante	famous	famoso(a)

ENGLISH	SPANISH
fascinate (to)	*fascinar*
favor	*favor*
favorite	*favorito(a)*
ferocious	*feroz*
finally	*finalmente*
firm	*firme*
flexible	*flexible*
flower	*flor*
fortunately	*afortunadamente*
fruit	*fruta*
funeral	*funeral*
furious	*furioso(a)*
G	
galaxy	*galaxia*
gallon	*galón*
garden	*jardín*
gas	*gas*
gasoline	*gasolina*
gigantic	*gigante*
giraffe	*jirafa*
glorious	*glorioso(a)*
golf	*golf*
gorilla	*gorila*
grade	*grado*
grand	*gran/grande*
group	*grupo*
guard	*guardia*
guardian	*guardián*
guide	*guía*
guitar	*guitarra*
gymnasium	*gimnasio*
gymnast	*gimnasta*
H	
helicopter	*helicóptero*
hippopotamus	*hipopótamo*
history	*historia*
honor	*honor*
hospital	*hospital*

ENGLISH	SPANISH
hotel	*hotel*
hour	*hora*
human	*humano(a)*
I	
idea	*idea*
identification	*identificación*
imagine (to)	*imaginar*
immediately	*inmediatamente*
immigrants	*inmigrantes*
importance	*importancia*
important	*importante*
impressed	*impresionando(a)*
impression	*impresión*
incredible	*increíble*
incurable	*incurable*
independence	*independencia*
information	*información*
insects	*insectos*
inseparable	*inseparable*
insist (to)	*insistir*
inspection	*inspección*
intelligence	*inteligencia*
interesting	*interesante*
interrupt (to)	*interrumpir*
introduce (to)	*introducir*
introduction	*introducción*
invent (to)	*inventar*
investigate (to)	*investigar*
invitation	*invitación*
invite (to)	*invitar*
island	*isla*
J	
jaguar	*jaguar*
K	
kangaroo	*canguro*
kilogram	*kilogramo*
L	
leader	*líder*

ENGLISH	SPANISH	ENGLISH	SPANISH
lemon	*limón*	**N**	
lens	*lente*	nation	*nación*
leopard	*leopardo*	natural	*natural*
lesson	*lección*	necessary	*necesario*
lessons	*lecciones*	necessity	*necesidad*
letter	*letra*	nectar	*néctar*
line	*línea*	nervous	*nervioso(a)*
lion	*león*	notice	*noticia*
list	*lista*	north	*norte*
locate (to)	*localizar*	number	*número*
M		**O**	
machine	*máquina*	obedience	*obediencia*
magic	*magia*	object	*objeto*
magician	*mago*	observatory	*observatorio*
magnificent	*magnífico(a)*	occasion	*ocasión*
manner	*manera*	ocean	*océano*
map	*mapa*	October	*octubre*
march (to)	*marchar*	office	*oficina*
March	*marso*	operation	*operación*
marionettes	*marionetas*	orbit	*orbita*
mathematics	*matemáticas*	orchestra	*orquesta*
medal	*medalla*	ordinary	*ordinario*
memory	*memoria*	**P**	
metal	*metal*	pajamas	*pijama*
microscope	*microscopio*	palace	*palacio*
million	*millón*	panic	*pánico*
miniature	*miniatura*	paper	*papel*
minute	*minuto*	park	*parque*
minutes	*minutos*	part	*parte*
modern	*moderno*	patience	*paciencia*
moment	*momento*	pear	*pera*
monster	*monstruo*	penguin	*pingüino*
monument	*monumento*	perfect	*perfecto(a)*
mountain	*montaña*	perfume	*perfume*
much	*mucho*	permanent	*permanente*
music	*música*	person	*persona*
museum	*museo*	petroleum	*petróleo*

ENGLISH	SPANISH
photo	*foto*
photograph	*fotografía*
photographer	*fotógrafo(a)*
piano	*piano*
pilot	*piloto*
pioneer	*pionero*
pirate	*pirata*
planet	*planeta*
planetarium	*planetario*
plans	*planes*
plants	*plantas*
plastic	*plástico*
plates	*platos*
poem	*poema*
police	*policía*
popular	*popular*
possible	*posible*
practice	*práctica*
practice (to)	*practicar*
prepare (to)	*preparar*
present (to)	*presentar*
present	*presente*
president	*presidente*
princess	*princesa*
problem	*problema*
professional	*profesional*

R	
radio	*radio*
ranch	*rancho*
really	*realmente*
rectangle	*rectangular*
restaurant	*restaurante*
retire (to)	*retirar*
reunion	*reunión*
rich	*rico(a)*
rock	*roca*
rose	*rosa*
route	*ruta*

ENGLISH	SPANISH
S	
sack	*saco*
sandals	*sandalias*
September	*septiembre*
series	*serie*
service	*servicio*
shampoo	*champú*
similar	*similar*
sofa	*sofá*
sound	*sonido*
special	*especial*
splendid	*espléndido(a)*
statistics	*estadística*
stomach	*estómago*
study (to)	*estudiar*
sum	*sumo*
surprise	*sorpresa*

T	
taxi	*taxi*
telephone	*teléfono*
telescope	*telescopio*
television	*televisión*
temperature	*temperatura*
terrible	*terrible*
theater	*teatro*
tiger	*tigre*
title	*titulo*
tomato	*tomate*
tone	*tono*
totally	*totalmente*
tourist	*turista*
traffic	*tráfico*
trap (to)	*atrapar*
tremendous	*tremendo*
triangle	*triangulo*
triple	*triple*
trumpet	*trompeta*
tube	*tubo*

ENGLISH	SPANISH
tunnel	*túnel*
U	
uniform	*uniforme*
V	
vegetables	*vegetales*
version	*versión*

ENGLISH	SPANISH
visit (to)	*visitar*
volleyball	*voleibol*
vote (to)	*votar*
Z	
zebra	*zebra*
zone	*zona*

Question Stems

Name _____ **Date** _____

Directions: Use this handout when you write questions for CSR. Question stems help make writing questions easier, so keep this handout in your CSR folder!

1. RIGHT THERE

Tip: Remember, an answer to a Right-There question is in *one* place in the text. You should be able to point to the answer and say, "It's right there!"

QUESTION STEMS FOR RIGHT-THERE QUESTIONS:

- Who was it that _____?
- What is _____?
- What was the turning point in _____?
- When did _____ happen?
- Where did _____ happen?
- How many _____ were there?

2. THINK AND SEARCH

Tip: Remember, an answer to a Think-and-Search question is in at least *two* places in the text. You have to look in two or more different places to find the answer.

QUESTIONS STEMS FOR THINK-AND-SEARCH QUESTIONS:

- Who was _____ and what did he (or she) do?
- What were some of the reasons for _____?
- What were some of the problems faced by _____?
- How was the problem of _____ solved?
- How are _____ and _____ different?
- How are _____ and _____ the same?

(continued)

Question Stems (continued)

3. AUTHOR AND YOU

Tip: Remember, an answer to an Author-and-You question is not entirely in the text. You have to think about what the author is telling you and what you already know. The answer to an Author-and-You question is in your head and in the text.

QUESTIONS STEMS FOR AUTHOR-AND-YOU QUESTIONS:

- What would you do if you were _____?
- What are the strengths (or weaknesses) of _____?
- When do you think _____ could happen again?
- Where has _____ ever happened before?
- Why is _____ a good or a bad thing?
- Why do you think _____ happened?
- How would you feel if _____?
- What do you think would have happened if _____?
- What else could we do to solve the problem of _____?
- What have you experienced similar to _____?

The Research Base Behind CSR

Researchers have conducted numerous studies of CSR over the years. Some of these have been quasi-experimental or experimental investigations of the effectiveness of CSR. Other studies have focused on different aspects of CSR, such as students' conversations while using CSR, or modified versions of CSR, such as computer-assisted CSR. We first describe CSR's precursor, a study of a modified version of reciprocal teaching. Then we present an overview of research studies on the effectiveness of CSR. Next we share lessons we have learned from three analyses of students' CSR discussions. We finish with a brief summary of a few other CSR studies.

CSR's Precursor

CSR is an extension of the reciprocal teaching research of Palincsar and Brown[1] and the collaborative group work of Johnson and Johnson.[2] CSR's precursor was a study on reciprocal teaching conducted as part of Klingner's dissertation[3] and later published[4] that included twenty-six seventh- and eighth-grade ELLs with LD. Following a reciprocal teaching format, small groups of students learned to use reciprocal teaching comprehension strategies (i.e., predicting, clarifying, summarizing, and questioning) in addition to brainstorming what they already knew about the topic of a day's passage. The purpose of brainstorming was to help them access prior knowledge. Participants discussed passages using Spanish and English. Once the majority of students were proficient in implementing the comprehension strategies, they either tutored younger peers in the strategies or participated in cooperative learning situations. Students in both groups made significant growth in reading comprehension on a standardized measure, the *Gates-MacGinitie Reading Test*.[5] Students with high oral language proficiency in both languages showed more improvement than students with lower oral language skills. Even students with low decoding abilities improved in reading comprehension. At the close of this study, one of the eighth-grade participants chided the researcher, "These are great strategies, but why did you wait so long to teach them to us? You should have taught them to us earlier, like in fourth grade!" Subsequent research studies did just that.

Quasi-Experimental and Experimental CSR Studies

The first quasi-experimental CSR research study occurred in heterogeneous, diverse fourth-grade classrooms in a large school.[6] The goal was to provide a feasible reading comprehension approach that would support the school's transition to an inclusive special education model. Accordingly, from its inception, CSR was intended to enhance content learning and active engagement as well as reading comprehension. The research team made multiple changes to reciprocal teaching in this study:

- Students only predicted once, before reading a day's passage, making an informed guess about what they thought they might learn after taking a peek at the passage and brainstorming what they knew about the topic.

- Students only generated teacherlike questions once, after reading an entire passage.

- Students used the clarifying strategy (referred to in CSR as *Click and Clunk*) and the main idea strategy (called *Get the Gist* in CSR) multiple times.

- Students learned the strategies during whole-class instruction and then applied them with expository text while working in small cooperative-learning groups.[7] In this first CSR study, students negotiated on the spot who would perform each cooperative-group role.

Researchers randomly assigned fourth-grade classes to the CSR condition or a typical instruction condition during social studies. CSR students made statistically significant greater gains than students in the control condition on the *Gates-MacGinitie Reading Test* (effect size = .44) and demonstrated equal proficiency in their knowledge of social studies content.

In another quasi-experimental study in culturally and linguistically diverse, inclusive, fourth-grade classrooms, researchers compared five CSR and five other teachers and their students, again during social studies.[8] Students in CSR classrooms improved significantly more in reading comprehension than comparison students on the *Gates-MacGinitie Reading Test* (effect sizes = .25 for high- and average-achieving students, .51 for low-achieving students, and .38 for students with LD). These effect sizes show that high- and average-achieving students, low-achieving students, and students with LD who learned CSR outperformed their counterparts who did not learn CSR, and that the greatest relative gains were made by low-achieving students. This finding suggests that CSR can help to close the achievement gap for struggling students.

The researchers also found that teachers varied in the quality and quantity of their CSR implementation and, with the exception of one teacher, that stronger CSR teachers' students showed greater gains in reading comprehension. The exception was the teacher who had the gifted and talented students in his class—these students were dispersed across CSR groups. Though the teacher frequently sat behind his desk rather than monitoring students' group work, thus earning lower fidelity of implementation scores,

TABLE B.1. CSR Quasi-Experimental and Experimental Research Studies, Effect Sizes on the *Gates-MacGinitie Reading Test*[9]

STUDY	DESIGN	PARTICIPANTS AND SETTING	EFFECT SIZES
Klingner, Vaughn, and Schumm (1998)	Quasi-experimental: Intact classes randomly assigned to condition (CSR or typical)	Fourth-grade students in large, culturally and linguistically diverse-inclusive classrooms at a range of achievement levels	$d = .44$ for total sample*
Klingner, Vaughn, Argüelles, Hughes, and Ahwee (2004)	Quasi-experimental: Intact classes randomly assigned to condition (CSR or typical)	Fourth-grade students in large, culturally and linguistically diverse, inclusive classrooms at a range of achievement levels	$d = .19$ for total sample*; .25 for high- and average-achieving students; .51 for low-achieving students; .38 for students with LD
Vaughn, Klingner, Swanson, Boardman, Roberts, Muhammed, and Stillman-Spisak (2011)	Experimental: Students randomly assigned to classes and classes randomly assigned to condition (CSR or typical); (teachers as their own controls)	Seventh- and eighth-grade students in diverse language arts or reading classrooms, with a focus on struggling readers	$g = .12$ for total sample*; .36 for struggling readers

*Statistically significant differences between CSR and non-CSR students in favor of CSR, $p \le .05$.

his students were excellent at using CSR and helping one another and showed high comprehension gains.

Based on this work with upper elementary students, we conducted an experimental study in diverse middle school language arts and reading classes.[10] Teachers served as their own controls, teaching CSR to students in randomly selected classes and providing students in other classes with "business as usual" instruction. Students in CSR classes scored statistically significantly higher than students in comparison classes on the *Gates-MacGinitie Reading Test* ($p = .05$) (effect sizes = .12 for the overall sample and .36 for struggling readers). Table B.1 describes the three studies with effect sizes on the *Gates-MacGinitie Reading Test*.

In a recent experimental study, Hitchcock et al. investigated the effectiveness of CSR with ELLs in seventy-four grade five social studies classrooms.[11] Using one outcome measure, the Group Reading Assessment and Diagnostic Evaluation (GRADE),[12] they found no statistically significant differences between groups in reading comprehension. Yet there were multiple problems with the way the study was carried out that limit its validity. Perhaps the biggest limitation of the study was a lack of fidelity. The researchers reported, "The single observation conducted for each classroom found that 21.6 percent of CSR teachers were using all five core teacher strategies, which the study defined as full procedural fidelity; 56.8 percent of teachers were observed using three or fewer strategies."[13] Most teachers appeared to be implementing CSR poorly and not very often. Thus, the study does not actually compare CSR with typical practice, but rather, something else—a weak substitute for CSR. Also, the researchers only observed teachers once, not enough times to get an accurate picture of their practice. Another concern is that the amount of professional development provided to teachers was less than what we consider adequate.

Valuable lessons can be learned from this study, however. The results support our assertion that for teachers to learn to implement reading comprehension strategies and cooperative learning well, high-quality, ongoing professional development is needed. Also, for students to realize gains with CSR, there may be a threshold in the quantity and quality of CSR that must be met, below which gains are less likely.

Students' Conversations During CSR

A notable feature of the Klingner, Vaughn, and Schumm study was that the researchers taperecorded students' discussions.[14] They wanted to understand students' interactions in CSR groups and the extent to which students focused on the application of strategies and on the content of their readings, and also on how well students supported one another during group work. They transcribed the discourse of one representative group per class, for a total of 1,325 utterances from sixteen sessions (with an utterance defined as a turn speaking regardless of length). They reported that 65 percent of discourse was academic in nature and content related, 25 percent was procedural, 8 percent was feedback, and 2 percent was off task. Students implemented the Click and Clunk and Get the Gist strategies the most consistently and effectively. Click and Clunk accounted for 52 percent of the strategy-related utterances. Students asked if anyone had a clunk, requested help with clunks, and provided explanations. In the following example, Maria is the group leader and Frank is persistent in seeking help:

Maria: Were there any clicks or clunks?

Frank: What is an economy?

Maria: An economy is when there's lots of workers and when they get together they make an economy. OK, is that it? Are there any more clunks? [attempting to move on]

Frank: I still don't know what economy is!

Maria: Lots of different people from different jobs working together . . .

Rita: . . . because they need money to pay the rent and buy a house and food and clothing?

Students discussed main ideas (gists) in what they were reading 25 percent of time. For the most part, students were able to state the gist of a paragraph accurately in their own words. However, good readers were much better at determining what was important than poorer readers and their gists tended to be more elaborate and more accurate than those of poorer readers. Students often tried to help each other with Get the Gist. Unlike with the previewing and clarifying strategies (with which students rarely helped each other, except by defining difficult words), peer assistance with the generation of more accurate or elaborate main ideas was common.

Groups varied in the extent to which everyone participated. Some leaders, but not all, made sure to call on everyone. Most group leaders ensured that each person contributed his or her ideas and would say something such as, "OK, anybody else want to say it in different words?"

Though students were able to apply the CSR strategies effectively, they were not focused enough on content. They spent excessive time on procedural discussions deciding who would perform what role in their groups. Also, too few higher-level discussions were noted among groups. Students sometimes assisted one another, but helping behaviors were uneven across groups. As a result, Klingner, Vaughn, and Schumm revised CSR to address these weaknesses.

Next, researchers implemented CSR in a fifth-grade class with thirty-eight bilingual English- and Spanish-speaking students and ELLs.[15] They investigated the frequency and manner by which students helped one another while using CSR in small, heterogeneous groups, hypothesizing that for cooperative learning to be effective, students must be able to assist one another consistently. Students received explicit instruction in how to provide assistance and work together. Rather than students deciding which roles to perform while working in their groups, the teacher determined roles and assigned students to the same groups, with the same roles, for multiple weeks at a time. Students applied CSR while reading their science textbook.

Researchers taperecorded and analyzed all student discourse from four lessons. This process yielded 4,072 utterances (speaking turns regardless of length), from forty-three sessions by six groups (encompassing approximately seventeen hours). Findings showed that overall, students spent very high amounts of time engaged in academic-related strategic discussion and assisted one another in understanding word meanings, getting the main idea, asking and answering questions, and relating what they were learning to previous knowledge. Each group provided some explanations in Spanish. All six groups spent approximately half of their total discussion time identifying and clarifying clunks. More variation was apparent in students' implementation of the Get the Gist and Wrap Up strategies. Wrap Up was applied the least consistently, in part because some groups usually ran out of time before finishing the day's reading.

For the most part, students were able to help one another, though the extent to which students did so varied across groups, and, within each group, some students were more proficient at providing assistance than others. In every group, bilingual students translated English vocabulary into Spanish, sometimes providing elaborate conceptual explanations of key vocabulary terms. They enabled and facilitated the language understanding of their classmates. In the following example, Carlos is the Clunk Expert.

Arelis:	What is vessels? Does anyone know?
Rafael:	Vessels go through the marrow and inside the bones.
Carlos:	Everyone find the word.
Arelis:	OK, where is it?
Carlos:	Umm, right here. OK, go right here, to the sentence before. Everyone put your finger over here where the word is. [Reading:] "Notice that vessels run into the marrow . . ." Look at the picture right here. And if you look up here, you see where it says "blood vessels." This is where the picture is helpful.
Rafael:	*Es una vena. Tú lo ves aquí. Es una vena que corre por el hueso. Es una vena de sangre. Es muy importante, el* blood vessel. *Es una vena que pasa por aquí.* [It's a vein. You see it here. It's a vein that runs through the bone. It's a blood vein. It's very important, the blood vessel. It's a vein that passes through here.]

Given how well the fifth-graders in this study supported one another, it appears that they received adequate instruction in how to collaborate and the right level of support to be successful. Also, the balance between strategies and content in student groups seemed optimal.

In the third discourse analysis,[16] researchers examined the discussions of the seventh- and eighth-grade students engaged in two experimental studies with CSR.[17] Klingner and colleagues audiotaped students' conversations twice in each class and found that students spent most of their time discussing clunks or figuring out gists. In fact, the number of utterances was almost exactly the same for each of these two strategies (926 and 925, respectively). Click and Clunk and Get the Gist were also the most often discussed strategies in previous CSR studies.

Students spent somewhat more time engaged in procedural discussions than the students in the Klingner and Vaughn study.[18] Procedural utterances varied a great deal. Many related to how to implement a strategy, particularly Question Generation, as in, "Do you guys know what those levels are (referring to QAR question types)? Do you know, Ricky (a student with LD)?" Some procedural utterances focused on roles, such as, "OK, who is the Question Expert?" And others pertained to the CSR process and what to do next, "Now it's time to Wrap Up." In a couple of classes, students seemed resistant to following a particular procedure, and the time figuring out what role to take or step to do next was borderline off-task behavior.

Students engaged in a balance of strategic and content-focused instruction and supported one another. They also were able to defend their ideas. They were mostly likely to evaluate each other's ideas and offer an alternative perspective when Getting the Gist. For example, in the following excerpt, students were trying to agree on the main idea of a passage:

Marcos:	Frederick Douglass married a white woman and died from a stroke, after . . .
Anna:	You've gotta put something about . . . [how] over the whole entire passage he stayed a strong abolitionist.
Seth:	Marrying a white person, or being with somebody white, it wasn't the main idea.
Marcos:	Yeah, but he . . .
Anna:	It's a key point, but it's not the main idea!

All of these examples of student discourse indicate what is possible when students work together to apply reading comprehension strategies and to assist one another to learn new content. Students at varying achievement levels and ELLs seem to have the support they need to participate and be successful. Yet, conversations such as these do not happen automatically. Professional developers, coaches, teachers, and students must put in the effort it requires to learn to implement CSR well. As one middle school teacher put it:

> It's a really good tool, but it takes work and you really have to put the work in for it to be successful. You do and so do the kids and they need to know that from the very beginning and if you're willing, you know, if you get your kids to get committed to it and you're committed to it, then, yeah, it can be a great thing. 'Cuz I mean, they're all wonderful reading strategies that you are trying to do anyway. This just kind of gives you extra support, I think, but it is a commitment. It is a commitment and you just have to kind of grin and bear it until you get there.

Other CSR Studies

In additional studies, Bryant et al. implemented CSR in an inclusive middle school and achieved gains for students with and without disabilities.[19] Vaughn et al. examined the effects of CSR on fluency and comprehension as part of a third-grade intervention, with positive results.[20] Kim et al. investigated a computer-adapted approach to using CSR in which students worked in pairs to read text on the computer and to implement CSR strategies.[21]

Theoretical Support for CSR

As noted, CSR is based primarily on theories and research on reading comprehension strategy instruction, particularly reciprocal teaching[22] and cooperative learning.[23] CSR has roots in cognitive psychology[24] as well as sociocultural theory.[25] Support for the value of teaching students metacognitive and cognitive strategies to aid their processing of text comes from cognitive psychology. The importance of peers working together and assisting one another to construct meaning derives from sociocultural theory.

One area of research with important implications for strategy instruction has used verbal protocols and think-alouds. By asking readers to think aloud while reading and processing text, it became apparent that good readers use comprehension strategies to support their understanding, often automatically, whereas poor readers typically do not.[26] Strategy instruction is based on the principle that poor comprehenders can improve their comprehension when they learn to apply the strategies used by good readers.[27]

Kintsch's reading comprehension model has had considerable impact on our thinking about CSR, especially in recent years.[28] Reading comprehension is an active process. Students engage with text by developing mental models that represent what they are reading. These mental models draw from the text as well as students' background knowledge and understanding of the purpose for reading. Efficient readers continuously fine-tune these mental models through an integrative process through which they resolve inconsistencies. In other words, when something in the text does not fit with existing mental models, readers revise them to incorporate new information.

Written words and how they are organized into sentences, paragraphs, and discourse units form a "textbase."[29] Readers connect their prior knowledge to the textbase to form a "situation model." Readers are most successful when there is a good match between the textbase and the situation model. A textbase that is too difficult for a student to read constrains this process. When readers struggle to read the words in a text, they may overrely on background knowledge and guess about what they are reading. Or readers who lack background knowledge may have a difficult time creating situation models that represent the text. Ideally, these are in balance.

Readers must ask themselves how what they read in one part of a text relates to information in another part of the text. They also must determine what is most important to remember. Readers continuously think about how new information they are reading relates to their prior knowledge. These are all strategies taught and reinforced by CSR. CSR supports students' comprehension in several ways emphasized by Kintsch: by making the textbase more accessible, by building relevant background knowledge needed to understand the text, by helping students establish connections between the text and their lives, by making the purpose for reading explicit, and by helping students identify the most information in the text and to synthesize ideas across paragraphs. It is this process that helps students develop a deep understanding of what they are reading and leads to learning. Kintsch wrote, "Text memory . . . may be achieved on the basis of only a superficial understanding. Learning from text, on the other hand, requires deep understanding."[30]

Over the years, we have learned to emphasize critical components of strategy instruction. The first three are similar to the principles delineated by Palincsar and Schutz.[31] First, the text is very important. Text that is too easy or too difficult or that does not lend itself well to the use of strategies does not support reading comprehension instruction. Also, as Palincsar and Schutz pointed out, reading multiple texts about the same topic is preferable to reading varied texts on distinct topics. Second, the focus of instruction must be on the content students are learning, with the strategies merely a way to support students' access to the content. Third, prior knowledge is very important. Not only should teachers help students activate existing background knowledge, they also should help students build new knowledge that will help them make sense of a text they will be reading. Fourth, when done well, Getting the Gist requires high-level thinking and promotes deep understanding. Students must synthesize important information across paragraphs in a section of text rather than merely conducting a quick check of surface-level understanding.

Factors That Influence Comprehension

Comprehension is influenced by many factors,[32] including characteristics of the reader, the text, the purpose of the task, and the learning environment. Characteristics of the reader that affect reading comprehension include interest and motivation, decoding skills, knowledge of structural analysis, vocabulary, prior knowledge, memory, use of comprehension strategies, and metacognition. Text features, such as the readability of the text and variations in text structure and organization, affect comprehension as well. The readability level of typical texts used in secondary classrooms may be too high for below-grade-level readers and the "unfriendliness" of many texts can result in comprehension challenges for students.[33] The learning environment is also important in affecting students' comprehension. When classrooms are well managed and provide a nurturing atmosphere where students feel safe, they are more likely to take risks and invest in learning.

NOTES

INTRODUCTION

1. J. K. Klingner, S. Vaughn, J. Dimino, J. S. Schumm, and D. Bryant, *Collaborative Strategic Reading: Strategies for Improving Comprehension* (Longmont, CO: Sopris West, 2001).

2. J. K. Klingner, S. Vaughn, M. E. Argüelles, M. T. Hughes, and S. Ahwee, "Collaborative Strategic Reading: 'Real World' Lessons from Classroom Teachers," *Remedial and Special Education, 25,* 2004, 291–302. J. K. Klingner, S. Vaughn, and J. S. Schumm, "Collaborative Strategic Reading During Social Studies in Heterogeneous Fourth-Grade Classrooms," *Elementary School Journal, 99,* 1998, 3–21. S. Vaughn, G. Roberts, J. K. Klingner, E. Swanson, A. Boardman, S. J. Stillman, S. Muhammed, and A. Leroux, "Collaborative Strategic Reading: Findings from Experienced Implementers" (under review).

CHAPTER 1: HOW CSR WORKS

1. Klingner et al. (2001).

2. T. E. Rafael, "Teaching Question Answer Relationships, Revisited," *The Reading Teacher,* February 1986, 516–522.

3. S. Kagan, "Cooperative Learning and Sociocultural Factors in Schooling," in California State Department of Education, *Beyond Language: Social and Cultural Factors in Schooling Language Minority Students* (Los Angeles: California State University, Evaluation, Dissemination and Assessment Center, 1986), pp. 231–298.

4. Ibid.

CHAPTER 2: TEACHING THE CSR STRATEGIES TO STUDENTS

1. This is an unpublished story written by Kathryn White.

2. S. Vaughn and J. K. Klingner, "Teaching Reading Comprehension Through Collaborative Strategic Reading," *Intervention in School and Clinic, 34,* 1999, 284–292.

3. Klingner et al. (2001).

4. Rafael (1986).

CHAPTER 3: IMPLEMENTING CSR COOPERATIVE LEARNING

1. D. Johnson and R. Johnson, *Learning Together and Alone* (5th ed.) (Edina, MN: Interaction Book Company, 2000).

2. These recommendations have been adapted from Klingner et al. (2001).

3. K. McMaster and D. Fuchs, "Cooperative Learning for Students with Disabilities," *Current Practice Alerts, 11,* 2005, 1–4.

4. See Klingner et al. (2001).

5. Ibid.

6. E. Aronson and S. Patnoe, *The Jigsaw Classroom: Building Cooperation in the Classroom* (2nd ed.) (New York: Addison Wesley Longman, 1997).

7. R. M. Gillies and M. Boyle, "Teachers' Discourse During Cooperative Learning and Their Perceptions of This Pedagogical Practice," *Teaching and Teacher Education, 24,* 2008, 1333–1348.

CHAPTER 4: USING STUDENT DATA TO INFORM INSTRUCTIONAL DECISIONS

1. J. Hattie and H. Timperley, "The Power of Feedback," *Review of Educational Research, 77,* 2007, 81–112.

2. Center on Instruction, *A Synopsis of Hattie & Timperley's "Power of Feedback"* (Portsmouth, NH: RMC Research Corporation, 2008).

3. This section on using data from learning logs has been adapted from A. G. Boardman, J. K. Klingner, A. Boele, and E. Swanson, "Collaborative Strategic Reading," in *Literacy and Learning: Advances in Learning and Behavioral Disabilities* (vol. 23), eds. T. Scruggs and M. Mastropieri (Bingley, UK: Emerald, 2010), pp. 205–235.

CHAPTER 5: PROVIDING CSR PROFESSIONAL DEVELOPMENT

1. L. M. Desimone, "Improving Impact Studies of Teachers' Professional Development: Toward Better Conceptualizations and Measures," *Educational Researcher, 38,* 2009, 181–199.

2. K. Beers, *When Kids Can't Read: What Teachers Can Do* (Portsmouth, NH: Heinemann, 2003).

3. C. Biancarosa and C. E. Snow, *Reading Next: A Vision for Action and Research in Middle and High School Literacy: A Report to Carnegie Corporation of New York* (2nd ed.). (Washington, DC: Alliance for Excellent Education, 2006). M. L. Kamil, G. D. Borman, J. Dole, C. C. Kral, T. Salinger, and J. Torgesen, *Improving Adolescent Literacy: Effective Classroom and Intervention Practices: A Practice Guide* (NCEE#2008-4027). (Washington, DC: National Center for Education Evaluation and Regional Assistance, Institute of Education Sciences, US Department of Education, 2008). Retrieved from http://ies.ed.gob/ncee/wwc.

4. A. L. Kindler, *Survey of the States' Limited English Proficient Students and Available Educational Programs and Services: 2000–2001 Summary Report* (Washington, DC: US Department of Education; Office of English Language Acquisition, Language Enhancement and Academic Achievement for Limited English Proficient Students, 2002). Retrieved from www.ncela.gwu.edu/states/reports/seareports/0001/sea0001 .pdf.

5. M. A. Mastropieri, T. E. Scruggs, and J. E. Graetz, "Reading Comprehension Instruction for Secondary Students: Challenges for Struggling Students and Teachers," *Learning Disability Quarterly, 26,* 2003, 103–116.

6. For the complete vignette, see Beers (2003).

7. For example, see A. S. Palincsar and A. L. Brown, "The Reciprocal Teaching of Comprehension-Fostering and Comprehension-Monitoring Activities," *Cognition and Instruction, 1,* 1984, 117–175.

8. For example, see D. Johnson and R. Johnson, *Cooperation and Competition: Theory and Research* (Edina, MN: Interaction Book Company, 1989).

9. Klingner, Vaughn, et al. (2004). Klingner, Vaughn, and Schumm (1998). Vaughn et al. (under review).

10. Johnson and Johnson (1989).

11. Colorín Colorado. (2007). *Using Cognates to Develop Comprehension in English.* Retrieved from www.colorincolorado.org/educators/background /cognates/.

12. M. Pressley, *Reading Instruction That Works: The Case for Balanced Teaching* (3rd ed.) (New York: The Guilford Press, 2006).

13. C. Q. Choi, "Less Bang, More Bubbles: Curtains of Air May Protect Fish from Noisy Human Activity," *Scientific American,* September 8, 2011. Retrieved from www.scientificamerican.com/article.cfm?id=less-bang-more-bubbles.

CHAPTER 6: SUPPORTING CSR THROUGH COACHING AND BOOSTER SESSIONS

1. B. F. Birman, L. Desimone, A. C. Porter, and M. S. Garet, "Designing Professional Development That Works," *Educational Leadership, 57,* 2000, 1–8.

2. Developed with support from grant #U396B100143, CSR-CO, funded by the U.S. Department of Education (2011).

3. J. Ellison and C. Hayes, *Cognitive Coaching: Weaving Threads of Learning into the Change of a Culture and Organization* (Norwood, MA: Christopher-Gordon Publishers, 2003).

APPENDIX A: CLASSROOM-READY CSR MATERIALS

1. Adapted from L. Diamond and L. Gutlohn, *Vocabulary Handbook* (Berkeley, CA: Consortium on Reading Excellence, 2006). S. Ebbers, *Language Links to Latin, Greek, and Anglo-Saxon: Increasing Spelling, Word Recognition, Fluency, Vocabulary, and Comprehension Through Roots and Affixes.* Presentation at the University of Texas Austin, 2005. S. Stahl and B. Kapinus, *Word Power: What Every Educator Needs to Know About Teaching Vocabulary* (Washington, DC: National Education Association, 2001).

2. Adapted from J. B. Carroll, P. Davies, and B. Richman, *The American Heritage Word Frequency Book* (Boston: Houghton Mifflin, 1971).

3. Ibid.

4. Adapted from Colorín Colorado (2007). Retrieved from www.colorincolorado.org /educators/background/cognates. Cognate list from the University of Texas Center for Reading and Language Arts "Third Grade Reading Academy," 2003.

APPENDIX B: THE RESEARCH BASE BEHIND CSR

1. Palincsar and Brown (1984).

2. Johnson and Johnson (1989).

3. J. K. Klingner, "Comprehensible Comments on Neuman and Koskinen (1992)," *Reading Research Quarterly, 28*, 1993, 376–382.

4. J. K. Klingner and S. Vaughn, "Reciprocal Teaching of Reading Comprehension Strategies for Students with Learning Disabilities Who Use English as a Second Language," *Elementary School Journal, 96*, 1996, 275–293.

5. W. H. MacGinitie and R. K. MacGinitie, *Gates-MacGinitie Reading Test* (3rd ed.) (Chicago: Riverside Publishing, 1989).

6. Klingner, Vaughn, and Schumm (1998).

7. See Dimino et al. (2001) for a more detailed description of the similarities and differences between reciprocal teaching and CSR.

8. Klingner, Vaughn, et al. (2004).

9. Klingner, Vaughn, and Schumm (1998). Klingner, Vaughn, et al. (2004). Vaughn, Klingner, et al. (in press).

10. S. Vaughn, J. K. Klingner, E. A. Swanson, A. G. Boardman, G. Roberts, S. S. Mohammed, and S. J. Stillman-Spisak, "Efficacy of Collaborative Strategic Reading with Middle School Students," *American Educational Research Journal, 48*, 2011, 938–954.

11. J. Hitchcock, J. Dimino, A. Kurki, C. Wilkins, and R. Gersten, *The Impact of Collaborative Strategic Reading on the Reading Comprehension of Grade 5 Students in Linguistically Diverse Schools* (NCEE 2011–4001). (Washington, DC: National Center for Education Evaluation and Regional Assistance, 2010).

12. K. T. Williams, *Group Reading Assessment and Diagnostic Evaluation (GRADE)* (Circle Pines, MN: American Guidance Service, 2001).

13. Hitchcock, Dimino, Kurki, Wilkins, and Gersten (2010), p. 3.

14. Klingner, Vaughn, and Schumm (1998).

15. J. K. Klingner and S. Vaughn, "The Helping Behaviors of Fifth-Graders While Using Collaborative Strategic Reading (CSR) During ESL Content Classes," *TESOL Quarterly, 34*, 2000, 69–98.

16. J. K. Klingner, A. G. Boardman, K. Scornavacco, A. Boelé, and S. Annamma, "Peer Discussions During Collaborative Strategic Reading Group Work." Presentation at the American Education Research Association Annual Meeting (New Orleans, 2011).

17. Vaughn, Klingner, et al. (2011). Vaughn, Roberts, et al. (under review).

18. Klingner and Vaughn (2000).

19. D. P. Bryant, S. Vaughn, S. Linan-Thompson, N. Ugel, A. Hamff, and M. Hougen, "Reading Outcomes for Students With and Without Reading Disabilities in General Education Middle-School Content Area Classes," *Learning Disability Quarterly, 23,* 2000, 238–252.

20. S. Vaughn, D. J. Chard, D. P. Bryant, M. Coleman, B. Tyler, S. Linan-Thompson, and K. Kouzekanani, "Fluency and Comprehension Interventions for Third-Grade Students," *Remedial and Special Education, 21,* 2000, 325–335.

21. A. Kim, S. Vaughn, J. K. Klingner, A. L. Woodruff, C. Klein, and K. Kouzekanani, "Improving the Reading Comprehension of Middle School Students with Disabilities Through Computer-Assisted Collaborative Strategic Reading (CACSR)," *Remedial and Special Education, 27,* 2006, 235–248.

22. Palincsar and Brown (1984).

23. Johnson and Johnson (1989).

24. J. H. Flavell, "Metacognition and Cognitive Monitoring: A New Area of Cognitive-Developmental Inquiry," *American Psychologist, 34,* 1979, 906–911.

25. B. Pérez, *Sociocultural Contexts of Language and Literacy* (Mahwah, NJ: Lawrence Erlbaum, 1998). S. Vygotsky, *Mind in Society* (Cambridge, MA: Harvard University Press, 1978).

26. F. R. Smith, "The Role of Prediction in Reading," *Elementary English, 52,* 1975, 305–311.

27. Kamil et al. (2008). M. Pressley and P. Afflerbach, *Verbal Protocols of Reading: The Nature of Constructively Responsive Reading* (Hillsdale, NJ: Erlbaum, 1995). S. Paris, B. Wasik, and J. Turner, "The Development of Strategic Readers," in eds. R. Barr, M. L. Kamil, P. Mosenthal, and P. D. Pearson, *Handbook of Reading Research* (vol. 2) (White Plains, NY: Longman, 1991), pp. 609–640.

28. W. Kintsch, *Comprehension: A Paradigm for Cognition* (New York: Cambridge University Press, 1998). W. Kintsch, "The Construction-Integration Model of Text Comprehension and Its Implications for Instruction," in eds. R. Ruddell and N. Unrau, *Theoretical Models and Processes of Reading* (5th ed.) (Newark, DE: International Reading Association, 2004).

29. W. Kintsch and T. A. van Dijk, "Toward a Model of Text Comprehension and Production," *Psychological Review, 85,* 1978, vol. 5, 363–394.

30. Kintsch (1998), p. 290.

31. A. S. Palincsar and K. M. Schutz, "Reconnecting Strategy Instruction with Its Theoretical Roots," *Theory into Practice, 50,* 2011, 85–92.

32. J. F. Carlisle and M. S. Rice, *Improving Reading Comprehension: Research-Based Principles and Practices* (Timonium, MD: York Press, 2002). RAND Reading Study Group, *Reading for Understanding. Toward an R&D Program in Reading Comprehension* (Santa Monica, CA: RAND Education, 2002).

33. Mastropieri, Scruggs, and Graetz (2003).

INDEX